My
Xbox® One

Bill Loguidice
Christina T. Loguidice

800 East 96th Street,
Indianapolis, Indiana 46240 USA

My Xbox® One

Copyright © 2014 by Pearson Education, Inc.

ISBN-13: 978-0-7897-5195-9
ISBN-10: 0-7897-5195-X

Library of Congress Control Number: 2014938085

Printed in the United States of America

First Printing: May 2014

Trademarks

All terms mentioned in this book that are known to be trademarks or service marks have been appropriately capitalized. Que Publishing cannot attest to the accuracy of this information. Use of a term in this book should not be regarded as affecting the validity of any trademark or service mark.

Xbox is a registered trademark of Microsoft Corporation.

Warning and Disclaimer

Every effort has been made to make this book as complete and as accurate as possible, but no warranty or fitness is implied. The information provided is on an "as is" basis. The authors and the publisher shall have neither liability nor responsibility to any person or entity with respect to any loss or damages arising from the information contained in this book.

Special Sales

For information about buying this title in bulk quantities, or for special sales opportunities (which may include electronic versions; custom cover designs; and content particular to your business, training goals, marketing focus, or branding interests), please contact our corporate sales department at corpsales@pearsoned.com or (800) 382-3419.

For government sales inquiries, please contact governmentsales@pearsoned.com.

For questions about sales outside the U.S., please contact international@pearsoned.com.

Editor-in-Chief
Greg Wiegand

Executive Editor
Loretta Yates

Development Editor
Todd Brakke

Managing Editor
Sandra Schroeder

Senior Project Editor
Tonya Simpson

Copy Editor
Karen Annett

Senior Indexer
Cheryl Lenser

Proofreader
Anne Goebel

Technical Editor
Mitchell Dyer

Editorial Assistant
Cindy Teeters

Book Designer
Anne Jones

Cover Designer
Mark Shirar

Compositor
Bumpy Design

Contents at a Glance

Table of Contents

4   Personalizing Your Xbox One Experience   115

5   Getting Your Game On   139

About the Authors

Bill Loguidice is a critically acclaimed technology author, as well as co-founder and managing director for the online publication, Armchair Arcade (www.armchairarcade.com). A noted video game and computer historian and subject matter expert, Bill personally owns and maintains more than 450 different systems from the 1970s to the present day, including a large volume of associated materials.

Bill is the author of the following major books: *Vintage Game Consoles: An Inside Look at Apple, Atari, Commodore, Nintendo, and the Greatest Gaming Platforms of All Time* (2014), *CoCo: The Colorful History of Tandy's Underdog Computer* (2013), *My PlayStation Vita* (2012), *My Xbox: Xbox 360, Kinect, and Xbox LIVE* (2012), *Motorola ATRIX For Dummies* (2011), *Wii Fitness For Dummies* (2010), and *Vintage Games: An Insider Look at the History of Grand Theft Auto, Super Mario, and the Most Influential Games of All Time* (2009).

Bill was also a writer and producer on the 2014 feature film documentary on the history of video games titled *Gameplay: The Story of the Videogame Revolution* and is hard at work on other exciting books, articles, and creative projects.

Christina Torster Loguidice is a scientific, technical, and medical (STM) editor and writer. Over her publishing career, she has overseen numerous peer-reviewed clinical journals and healthcare technology magazines. Christina is currently the editorial director of *Annals of Long-Term Care: Clinical Care and Aging*, a monthly, peer-reviewed, clinical journal dedicated to improving the care of long-term care residents. She is also a contributing editor on the clinical journal, *Consultant*, and reports from several medical conventions annually.

Christina is the author of the following major books: *Cancer Nutrition and Recipes For Dummies* (2013), *My PlayStation Vita* (2012), *My Xbox: Xbox 360, Kinect, and Xbox LIVE* (2012), and *Wii Fitness For Dummies* (2010).

Christina is also the developer and course instructor for the online course *Explore a Career in Medical Writing*. She also served as a production assistant on the 2014 feature film, *Gameplay: The Story of the Videogame Revolution*, a documentary on the history of video games.

Dedications

Bill and Christina:
To our new niece, Jenna Josephine Renzi, with all of our love.

Christina:
To my Onkel Pete and Tante Astrid. Thank you for being such amazing people and for all the wonderful times spent with you in the Berkshires. The lovely memories will reside with me forever.

Acknowledgments

Thanks as always to everyone at Pearson Education and Que for their professionalism and assistance with this project, including Loretta Yates, Todd Brakke, and Tonya Simpson. Special thanks to our technical reviewer, Mitchell Dyer, and our literary agent, Matt Wagner.

We Want to Hear from You!

As the reader of this book, *you* are our most important critic and commentator. We value your opinion and want to know what we're doing right, what we could do better, what areas you'd like to see us publish in, and any other words of wisdom you're willing to pass our way.

We welcome your comments. You can email or write to let us know what you did or didn't like about this book—as well as what we can do to make our books better.

Please note that we cannot help you with technical problems related to the topic of this book.

When you write, please be sure to include this book's title and authors as well as your name and email address. We will carefully review your comments and share them with the authors and editors who worked on the book.

Email: feedback@quepublishing.com

Mail: Que Publishing
ATTN: Reader Feedback
800 East 96th Street
Indianapolis, IN 46240 USA

Reader Services

Visit our website and register this book at quepublishing.com/register for convenient access to any updates, downloads, or errata that might be available for this book.

Prologue: Getting to Know the Xbox One

This book explains how to tap into the powerful features of the Xbox One so it can take its rightful place as the centerpiece of your home entertainment system. Despite its name, the Xbox One is actually Microsoft's third console, after the Xbox, which debuted on November 15, 2001, and the Xbox 360, which debuted on November 22, 2005.

The Xbox One debuted on November 22, 2013. It proved an immediate hit, selling more than 1 million consoles in the first 24 hours of its rollout, spanning just 13 initial countries. The Xbox One represents a fresh start for Microsoft because none of the games or accessories for their previous consoles work with the new system. In fact, the Xbox One interface has more in common with the Windows 8 and Windows Phone operating systems than it does with even the latest version of the Xbox 360.

Understanding the Prerequisites

The Xbox One breaks from the tradition set by previous generations of consoles by only working with one type of display, a minimum 720p high-definition or better television or monitor with an HDMI input. Fortunately, most televisions sold within at least the last 5 to 10 years meet this requirement, and, if for some reason you don't already have one, you can get large, 1080p-capable displays for little more than what you paid for your console. Likewise, although not strictly a requirement, the Xbox One can take great advantage of a quality sound system either through its HDMI Out or S/PDIF (optical audio) ports.

What About 4K Ultra HD?

Compared with standard high-definition televisions (HDTVs) that have a maximum resolution of 1920×1080, 4K Ultra HD displays have a maximum resolution of 3840×2160, as well as an increased color gamut. For now, both the exorbitant prices of these 4K displays and the lack of content that takes advantage of the increased resolution puts Ultra HD capabilities out of the reach of the average consumer. Impressively, both the Xbox One itself and the high-quality HDMI cable that it comes with support 4K Ultra HD displays, so if you do end up eventually getting such a television, your console will support it. Keep in mind, however, that "support" and having actual content natively in that resolution are two very different things. At this time, no Xbox One games display at 4K resolution, and it's unlikely that any games will display at 4K resolution in the near future.

Of all the new features in Xbox One, one of the most impressive is its capability to integrate your cable or satellite box with it. Although a cable or satellite receiver box is not required, the HDMI In on your console would be awfully lonely without it. The benefit of connecting such a box to your Xbox One is that not only can you reuse the primary HDMI input on your television (freeing other inputs for other devices), but you can also enhance the use of your cable or satellite service. If your cable or satellite receiver box does not presently connect to your television via HDMI, then you must contact your service provider for a newer model that the Xbox One can take advantage of.

It's Not All Good

It might be tempting to use the Xbox One's HDMI In for something other than a cable or satellite receiver box, such as an Xbox 360. Unfortunately, the pass-through chaining process introduces a slight delay that might impact devices like other video game consoles that depend on near-instantaneous response when a controller command is issued. As such, it's best to use the HDMI In for devices that only play video.

Finally, although an existing wired or wireless network is not strictly a requirement after initial setup is finished, you're limited to playing only retail game discs unless you go online. Similarly, without an Xbox Live Gold account (see Chapter 3, "Examining Xbox Live"), access to the most interesting Xbox One features, like many of the video and music services, Skype video chat, and online gameplay, are not available.

Unboxing Your Xbox One

Freeing your Xbox One from its box can be an exhilarating, but somewhat tedious process. All Xbox One packages come with, at minimum, the console, Kinect sensor, wireless controller and AA batteries, chat headset, 6.5-foot (2-meter) HDMI cable, power supply and power cord, and various documents, so there are plenty of items to extract. Luckily, no tools are required for removing and setting up your system other than your hands and some patience.

However, before you start trying to hook up the Xbox One to your TV, sound system, or cable or satellite receiver box, it's wise to familiarize yourself with all of its parts so that you can plan accordingly. For instance, you ultimately want to place your Xbox One console in a location where it's both stable and there's enough clearance around the unit to ensure none of its ventilation openings are blocked. You also need to make similar arrangements for the Kinect sensor, along with providing it a clear view of your living space. If a wireless Internet connection is not available, you want to place your console close enough to make a wired connection to your home network; otherwise, you'll have to make do without many of the connected features that make the Xbox One so great. Nevertheless, even if you choose to eschew online features and just want to play disc-based games, you still need a broadband Internet connection for first-time setup to download an initial update before your shiny new console will even let you play.

Breaking Down the Components

Each of the components included in the Xbox One's box has a variety of connectors or inputs, as well as a range of other features. Familiarizing yourself with these major features makes setup and use easier.

Xbox One Console

Your Xbox One includes a variety of buttons and ports, located on the front, left, and rear of the console. Inside the console is a 500GB hard drive, which gives you plenty of storage space for game downloads, movie and music purchases, and so on. Of course, eventually, even that much storage space will become cramped, so it's nice to know that Microsoft plans to add support for external hard drives, attached via one of the Xbox One's three USB ports, in the future.

Now, let's review the features on the front of the Xbox One console:

- **Disc slot**—This is where you load and unload a Blu-ray, DVD, or audio CD disc. Once a disc is inserted part of the way into the slot, it is automatically pulled into the console and read.

- **Eject button**—Press this button to eject a disc that is inside the console.

- **Xbox button**—This is the power button and LED status indicator.

- **Cooling vent**—This vent allows heat to escape from your console. This vent should never be blocked.

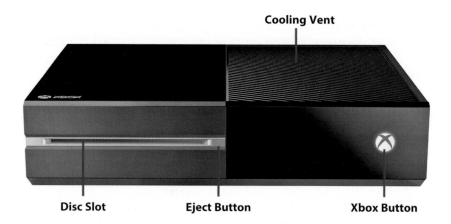

Now take a look at the features on the left side of the Xbox One console:

- **USB 3.0 port**—Use this port to connect wired accessories, such as the Xbox One Play & Charge Kit (see "Accessorizing Your Xbox One" in Chapter 4, "Personalizing Your Xbox One Experience").

- **Eject hole**—If a disc ever gets stuck in your console, you can use this to manually eject it. See "Manually Eject Discs" in Chapter 1, "Setting Up Your Xbox One," for how to use the eject hole.

- **Accessory Pairing button**—Press this button when you want to connect additional wireless accessories, such as a wireless controller, to your console.

- **Cooling vent**—This vent allows heat to escape from your console. This vent should never be blocked. Similarly, the entire right side of the console has a cooling vent.

Accessory pairing button

Cooling vent   **USB 3.0 port**   **Eject hole**

Keeping Your System Clean

One way to help maintain your Xbox One and its components in top working condition is to keep dust out of and off of them. Although not strictly necessary, before cleaning your console or any of its components, unplug all connections. Only use a dry microfiber cloth to remove dust, as liquids or other materials may damage the finish or internal components.

Finally, take a look at the features on the rear of the Xbox One console:

- **Power supply port**—The power supply plugs directly into this port.

- **HDMI Out**—One end of the included HDMI cable plugs into here, while the other end plugs into your television. See "Hook Up Your Xbox One" in Chapter 1 for more information on connecting to your television.

- **S/PDIF**—This port provides optical audio output, which is typically used to connect to sound systems. An optical audio cable is not included. See "Display & Sound" in Chapter 2, "Navigating Your Xbox One's Dashboard and Settings," for more information on connecting to a sound system.

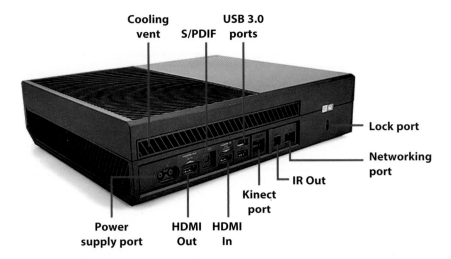

- **HDMI In**—The HDMI cable from your cable or satellite receiver box optionally plugs in to here. See Chapter 1 for more information on connecting a cable or satellite receiver box.

- **USB 3.0 ports**—USB stands for *universal serial bus*. These ports enable you to attach peripheral devices to your console, such as a wired controller or, eventually, a flash or hard drive for additional storage capacity. Your console has three of these ports, one on the side and two in back.

- **Kinect port**—This is the dedicated Kinect USB port, handling both data and power for this motion and voice control camera device.

- **IR Out**—This is an infrared (IR) output port for connecting an optional IR blaster. See "Accessorizing Your Xbox One" in Chapter 4 for more information on IR blasters.

- **Networking port**—This is an Ethernet, or network, port, allowing for a wired connection.

- **Lock port**—This port enables you to connect a laptop lock to keep your console secured in areas where physical security may be an issue. See "Accessorizing Your Xbox One" in Chapter 4 for more on what to use with the lock port.

- **Cooling vent**—This vent enables heat to escape from your console. This vent should never be blocked.

Kinect Sensor

The new Kinect sensor offers several improvements over its predecessor for the Xbox 360, including a wide-angle lens, nearly three times the resolution, and the capability to see in the dark thanks to an active IR sensor. It also can see objects that are closer to the sensor (within 3 feet) and track up to six different bodies (skeletons) at once. Other new features include the capability to detect a player's heart rate, facial expressions, 25 individual joints (even fingers!) and the precise rotation of those joints, weight put on each limb, and speed of movements, as well as the capability to track gestures performed with the wireless controller. It's also an IR blaster, so it can control your cable or satellite receiver box, television, and sound system.

Kinect's microphone remains active at all times, so it's always ready to receive voice commands from the user when needed, even when the console is in Sleep mode (but not when it is powered off). Although it's not necessary to keep Kinect active or even plugged in, if you don't, you'll clearly be missing out on some interesting functionality.

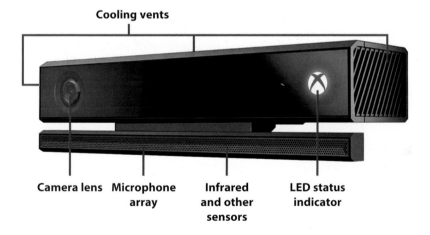

Cooling vents

Camera lens   Microphone   Infrared   LED status
array   and other   indicator
sensors

Wireless Controller

How do you follow up the Xbox 360's controller when it was already considered one of the greatest ever made? Simple—keep just about everything that was so great about it, improve upon its weaknesses (the D-pad), and then add new features such as faster response time, impulse triggers that deliver precise vibration feedback, and infrared LEDs that can be tracked by Kinect. Best of all, up to eight of these new Xbox One controllers can be paired to one console (with Kinect keeping track of who's who), making for some crazy local multiplayer sessions for games that support it.

Now, take a look at the features of the Xbox One wireless controller:

Understanding Digital and Analog

You'll hear a lot about *digital* and *analog* when it comes to your controller. Digital uses discrete values and analog uses a continuous range of values. The digital D-pad and buttons register as on or off. For example, with the D-pad, if you move an in-game character left, it simply moves left. The analog sticks and triggers allow for a finer degree of control. For example, with the analog stick, you can control how quickly an in-game character moves left.

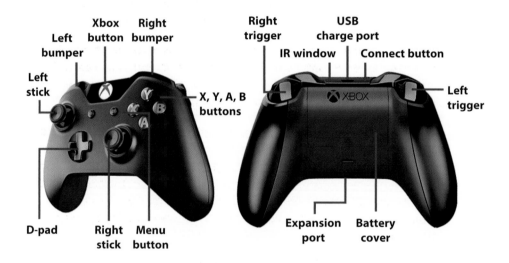

- **Left stick**—The primary analog control stick, which functions much like a D-pad, but due to its analog nature (detecting minute movements) is not as precise when navigating menus. It also functions as a button when you press down on it, often bringing up secondary functions or in-game menus.

- **Left and right bumpers**—Digital buttons that often act as quick scroll buttons in menu screens, with the right bumper scrolling right and the left bumper scrolling left.

- **Xbox button**—A digital button with a wide range of functions. If the console is off (LED status indicator off), hold this button to turn on the console. If the console is already on and the controller is off (LED status indicator off), hold this button to turn on the controller. If both the console and controller are already on, hold this button down to bring up the option to turn off the console or controller. With both the controller and console on, press this button at any time to show the Home screen (see Chapter 2). Finally, when viewing two snapped apps, where you move one to the right side of your screen while you do something else on the main part of your screen, press this button twice in rapid succession to toggle between the two apps.

- **X, Y, A, B buttons**—Digital buttons that can serve any assigned menu or in-game function. Typical usage for the X button is to cancel or exit a selection. Typical usage for the Y button is to bring up a menu. Typical usage for the A button is to accept selections. Typical usage for the B button is to go back to a previous screen or exit a screen.

- **D-pad**—A digital control that provides eight-directional input, enabling you to go up, down, left, right, up and left, up and right, down and left, and down and right. Some games do not allow use of the D-pad for movement but map certain in-game functions to it.

- **Right stick**—The secondary analog stick, often used to look around and adjust the camera angle in games that provide this functionality. It is also sometimes used for moving around in games, though use of the left stick for this function is much more common. The right stick also functions as a button. For example, in games that enable you to adjust the camera angle, pressing the button might return the camera's vantage point to the center.

- **View button**—A digital button used to focus in on an activity in a game or app, such as accessing the address bar in Internet Explorer (see Chapter 10, "Surfing with Internet Explorer"). The function of this button varies depending on the app or game, with some completely ignoring its existence.

- **Menu button**—A digital button to access game- and app-specific menu options, such as Settings or Help, along with commands within the user interface, such as pressing the equivalent of Enter on a keyboard.

- **Right and left triggers**—Analog buttons that act as up and down quick scroll buttons in menu screens, with the left trigger scrolling down and the right trigger scrolling up. These are also called impulse triggers, which means they can feature rumble effects during gameplay.

- **IR window**—Infrared LEDs that are hidden behind the smoked plastic cover. These help Kinect see the controller and are used for auto-pairing controllers to the console (see "Assigning a Profile to a Wireless Controller" in Chapter 4).

- **USB charge port**—A Micro-USB port used to connect a USB cable to the controller for charging the optional Xbox One Play & Charge Kit or third-party equivalent (see "Accessorizing Your Xbox One" in Chapter 4). With a USB to Micro-USB cable plugged between the console and controller, the controller can also act like a wired controller, with no need for batteries.

- **Connect button**—A button used to sync a controller with a new or different Xbox One console (see "Connecting Additional Controllers" in Chapter 1).

- **Battery cover**—A cover for the compartment where the included AA batteries go.

- **Expansion port**—An accessory port, used to attach add-ons like the included Xbox One chat headset.

Chat Headset

The included headset enables you to chat with friends and family in both party chat (see Chapter 6, "Making the Social Connection") and supported online multiplayer games (see Chapter 5, "Getting Your Game On"). Now take a look at the features of the Xbox One chat headset:

- **Earpiece**—Enables you to hear friends and family.

- **Microphone**—Enables your friends and family to hear you. The whole earpiece and microphone assembly rotates to accommodate use on the left or right ear.

- **Expansion port connector**—Plugs in to the expansion port on the Xbox One wireless controller to establish and secure a connection.

- **Mute**—Mutes your microphone so that others can no longer hear you.

- **Volume up/down**—Increases (when you press +) or decreases (when you press –) the volume you hear in the earpiece.

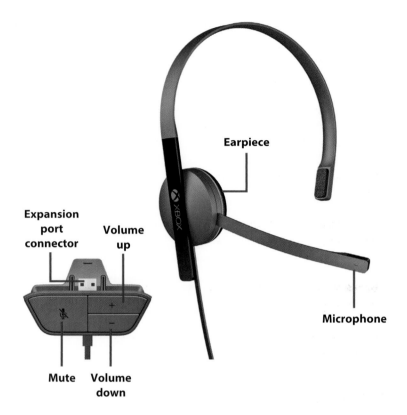

What to Expect from This Book

We wrote this book with few assumptions made about reader skill level
or any preliminary understanding of its many topics. If something needs
explaining, we explain it. Although you can skip to a chapter of interest, each
chapter does build upon what came before it. In this way, if you read the
book from its first chapter to its last, you can be assured that you'll be armed
with all you need to know about the Xbox One. With such a foundation, you
can more easily understand and make great use of any new Xbox One features Microsoft adds over the years.

**Learn to position, set up, and
configure your new home
entertainment centerpiece**

In this chapter, you learn about setting up and starting to use your Xbox One and its related attachments and components.

Setting Up Your Xbox One

In this chapter, you learn about positioning and setting up your Xbox One console, Kinect, and other components, such as the wireless controller. This setup includes connecting to your home network and cable or satellite receiver box, as well as configuring key settings. Luckily, none of this is particularly difficult, so you'll be on your way to playing games, watching videos, and having all kinds of other Xbox One fun in no time.

Making a Home for Your Xbox One

If you read this book's Prologue, "Getting to Know the Xbox One," you have a good handle on all of your Xbox One's parts, so now it's just about time to hook up everything so that you can start enjoying your new system. That process won't take long, provided you secure a proper place for your console, power supply, and Kinect and don't have to move heavy furniture or lots of dusty knickknacks out of the way.

Many wall units or entertainment centers that have their component shelves behind glass or wooden doors don't make good homes for sensitive electronic equipment like the Xbox One. Many times, the only available air holes are circular cutouts in the back of the unit or center for cable routing. If you have a unit or center like this, at minimum, increase the number of air holes, or optimally, place the Xbox One in a more open area.

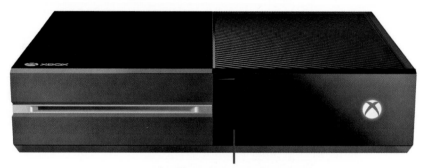

**The Xbox One console must sit
horizontally on a stable surface
with good ventilation**

Unlike the Xbox 360, which could be placed vertically, the Xbox One is designed for only horizontal placement on a flat, stable surface so that the console doesn't wobble. The console's cooling vents should have sufficient clearance for proper airflow. Similarly, to maximize air ventilation and minimize heat, the Xbox One should not be placed on any objects nor have any objects placed on it.

The included HDMI cable is approximately 6.5 feet long (2 meters), so your console must be well within that distance of your television's or sound system's HDMI input. If you plan to connect your cable or satellite receiver box to your Xbox One's HDMI In, it also must be within range of your console. Under that scenario, where the HDMI connection already exists for your cable or satellite box, you can simply unplug the existing HDMI cable from the back of your box and plug it in to the Xbox One's HDMI Out. You can then use the Xbox One's included HDMI cable to go from the cable or satellite receiver box's HDMI Out into the console's HDMI In.

Need More Length?

Longer HDMI cables are available from a variety of retail outlets. These cables should work just as well as the high-quality HDMI cable that's included with your Xbox One as long as it's of reasonable quality and doesn't exceed 25 feet in length.

The Xbox One's external power supply features a built-in fan and has similar ventilation requirements as the console. Ideally, you should plug in the power cord to a grounded, surge-protected power strip or equivalent, but any open outlet will suffice.

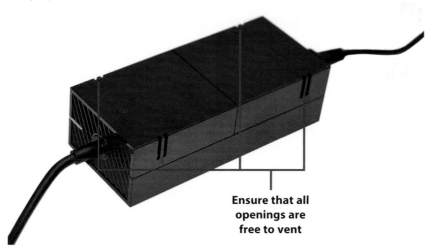

**Ensure that all
openings are
free to vent**

It's Not All Good

Heat Damage

Although your console shuts off automatically if it doesn't have sufficient ventilation, regular overheating can ultimately lead to a damaged system and the need for a service call (see the "Understanding Your Warranty" section later in this chapter). This is why it's best to plan ahead and make every consideration for achieving many years of trouble-free usage.

The Kinect sensor has a 9-foot (3-meter) cable that plugs in to the Kinect port on the back of the console. Because there is no way to extend the cable's length, the Kinect must be well within 9 feet of the console. Like the console, the Kinect sensor must be placed horizontally on a level, stable surface with plenty of ventilation. The Kinect sensor also must have an unobstructed view of your play space and floor.

The Kinect sensor has to sit in a horizontal position on a stable surface with good ventilation and an unobstructed view of your play area

Kinect should be between 2 and 6 feet (0.6–1.8 meters) from the floor. Because of its wide-angle lens, its capability to see your play space generally improves the higher it's placed. Although the Kinect sensor can be positioned below your television, ideal placement is approximately 6 inches (15 centimeters) above your display (see "Accessorizing Your Xbox One" in Chapter 4, "Personalizing Your Xbox One Experience," for television-mounting options). Whenever possible, have the Kinect sensor avoid direct sunlight, which might impair its tracking capability. Similarly, try to keep the sensor at least 1 foot away from any speakers, which might impair its capability to hear voice commands.

Hook Up Your Xbox One

Now that you've secured positions for your Xbox One, power supply, and Kinect, it's time to get it all connected. Follow these steps:

1. Remove the stickers from the front and back of the console.

Sticker Removal

You might find it odd to remove the rear sticker, what with the helpful labels above each port, but this recommendation comes straight from Microsoft.

2. Connect the included HDMI cable to the HDMI Out port on your console. Alternatively, if you're connecting your cable or satellite receiver box to your Xbox One, unplug the HDMI cable from the HDMI Out on the box and plug it in to the HDMI Out port on your console.

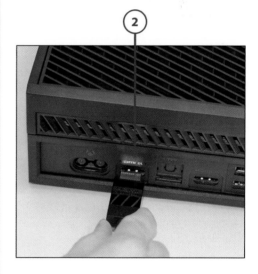

   If you've connected your cable or satellite receiver box, proceed to step 3; otherwise, proceed to step 4.

Before You Connect

Make sure to remove the protective plastic from both ends of the included HDMI cable before you connect it.

3. Connect the included HDMI cable to the HDMI Out of your cable or satellite receiver box to the HDMI In on the console. Proceed to step 5.

4. Plug in the other end of the HDMI cable connected to the console's HDMI Out to an HDMI input on your television or sound system.

    If you have a sound system that only supports S/PDIF, connect an optical audio cable (not included) from the Xbox One's S/PDIF output to the sound system's input.

5. If you are connecting your Xbox One directly to a cable modem, network port, or router, connect a networking cable (not included) from an open port on the respective device to the console's networking port. Otherwise, if you plan on using the Xbox One's wireless networking option, proceed to step 6.

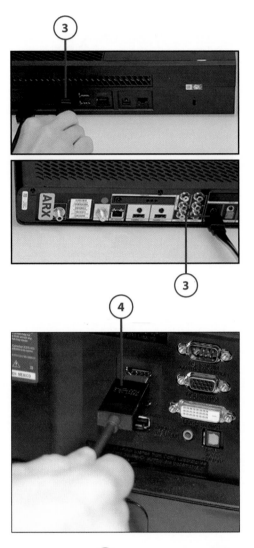

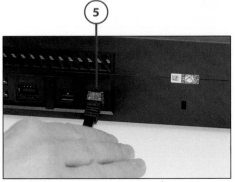

6. Remove the protective plastic from the Kinect sensor and power supply as well as the end cap from the Kinect's cable.

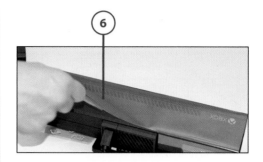

7. Connect the Kinect's cable to the console's Kinect port.

8. Plug in the power supply to the power supply port on the console.

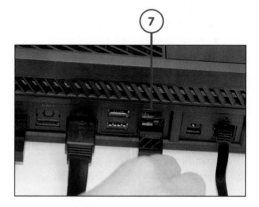

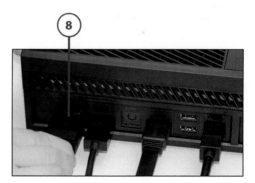

9. Plug in the power cord to the power supply.

10. Plug in the other end of the power cord to an electrical outlet. The LED on the power supply should be amber, indicating that there's power but the console is not yet turned on.

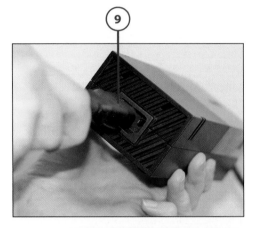

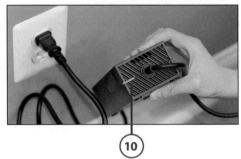

Power On for the First Time

Now that all of the necessary connections have been made, it's time to power on for the first time and begin the onscreen setup. Follow these steps:

1. Turn on your television and sound system (if applicable). Make sure your display is on the same input that the Xbox One is connected to (usually HDMI 1).

   If you connected your Xbox One to a sound system over S/PDIF, make sure the sound system is also on the correct source.

2. Remove the battery cover on the wireless controller, insert the included AA batteries with the correct polarity (+/-) into the battery compartment, and replace the battery cover.

3. Press the Xbox button on the controller. Your console turns on.

4. After a short loading sequence, the controller activation screen appears. Press the A button on your controller.

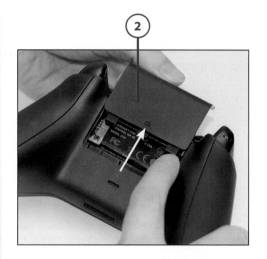

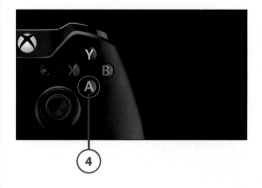

5. Move the D-pad or left stick up or down if you need to select a language other than English. Press the A button when your chosen language is highlighted to select it.

6. Move the D-pad or left stick up or down the list of countries and press the A button when your chosen country is highlighted.

7. Press the A button to continue. If you are using a wired connection, proceed to step 10. If you are using a wireless connection, move the D-pad or left stick up or down to select an available wireless network. If your wireless network is not listed, for instance if its SSID is set to hidden, select Add Wireless Network to manually enter its name. Once your selection is highlighted, press the A button.

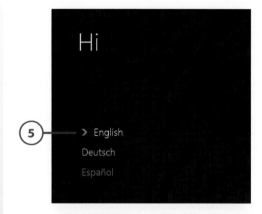

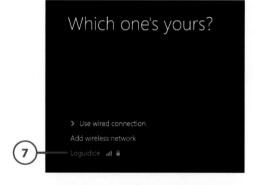

It's Not All Good

Knowing Your TV

In rare cases, the Xbox One might not be able to automatically determine your TV's resolution. If this happens, a Change Your Display option appears. Select either 720p or 1080p, depending on your TV's capabilities.

8. Enter your network's password using the D-pad or left stick, selecting each letter with the A button. Press the left stick like a button to turn on capital letters, and use the left trigger to turn on symbols. Press either one again to go back to regular lowercase text input. When you are finished entering your password, press the Menu button or select Enter on the onscreen keyboard.

9. If you successfully connected, you'll see You're Connected. Press the A button to continue; otherwise, press the B button to go back and try again.

10. Press the A button to start the system update, which ensures your new console has access to all of the latest system features. Your screen might temporarily go black and your console might restart one or more times during the update.

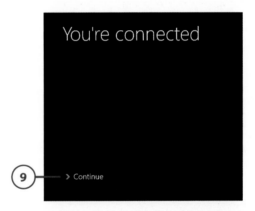

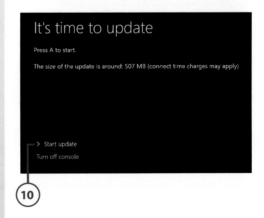

11. After your console restarts and prompts you onscreen, press the Xbox button on your controller.

12. Press the A button to select your time zone. Move up and down between the selections with the D-pad or left stick. Press the A button to make your selection.

13. Use the D-pad or left stick down to select Next. Press the A button.

14. To begin Kinect setup, press the A button, then continue to the next step. If you don't want to set up Kinect, select Skip instead and skip to step 17.

Choose your time zone

(UTC-05:00) Eastern Time (US & Canada)

✔ Automatically adjust for daylight saving

Next

Ⓐ Select

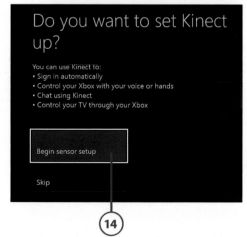

Do you want to set Kinect up?

You can use Kinect to:
• Sign in automatically
• Control your Xbox with your voice or hands
• Chat using Kinect
• Control your TV through your Xbox

Begin sensor setup

Skip

15. Position yourself so that Kinect can see you. Press the A button.

16. Make sure your speakers are turned up to above normal levels. Press the A button to begin the audio check. Try to stay as quiet as possible for each consecutive test. When the audio tests are complete, press the A button twice to proceed to setting up an account.

17. Press the A button to continue sign-in with either an existing or new Microsoft account. Valid accounts include Microsoft products and services like Xbox Live, Skype, Outlook.com, Hotmail.com, Live.com, Windows Phone, and Windows 8, though email addresses from other services will also work.

18. Use the onscreen keyboard to enter your credentials from an existing Microsoft account. If you don't have a Microsoft account, enter your main email address from any other email service, which then becomes associated with a new Microsoft account. Press the Menu button or select Enter on the onscreen keyboard to proceed.

If you'd rather get a new email address to use for your Microsoft account, press the B button on the controller and select Get a New Email to open a new Outlook.com email account.

Follow the remaining onscreen prompts and instructions.

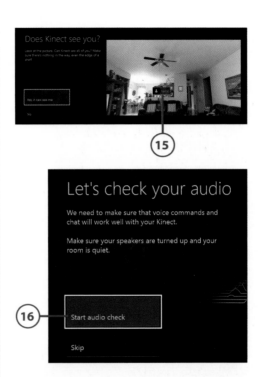

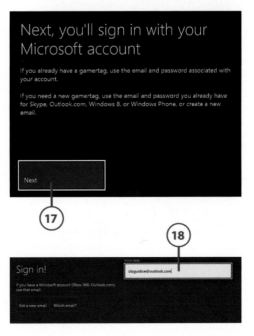

19. Read and accept the Xbox Terms of Use and privacy statement. Decide whether to enable or disable the sending of promotional offers and the sharing of your contact info. When you're satisfied with the settings, select I Accept. Do the same for the privacy statement that appears next.

20. Choose a color theme (this can be changed later; see "Customizing Your Profile" in Chapter 4 for more information), then select Next.

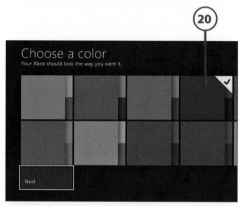

21. You see how you appear on this Xbox One console and when connected on Xbox Live. The gamerpic and gamertag can be changed later (see Chapter 4). Select Next.

22. If you're concerned about the security of your Xbox One at your present location, select Keep Asking for My Password. Otherwise, select Save My Password, which automatically logs you in.

    If you do decide you want additional security, you can create a six-digit passkey later on (see "Changing the Console Settings" in Chapter 2).

23. Choose to automatically or manually sign in with Kinect. Choosing to sign in automatically with Kinect enables your Xbox One to recognize and log you in when you enter the room. If you choose this option, you are asked to verify that the sensor has identified you.

(23)

24. Select That's Me after you're successfully identified. If you're not immediately recognized, raise your hand above your head.

25. Press the A button to continue past the Xbox Live Gold preview screen.

(24)

(25)

26. Decide which Xbox Live Gold membership term you'd like (see Chapter 3, "Examining Xbox Live," for more on Xbox Live Gold). Your console most likely came with a promo code for a free trial period (typically 14 days), which can be activated by selecting Use a Code and following the instructions. If you don't want to activate Xbox Live Gold, select No Thanks, which gives you an Xbox Live Free account and restricts many of the console's online features.

Already Golden?

If you already have an Xbox Live Gold account associated with an Xbox 360, you can continue to use that account for your Xbox One.

27. A short introductory video plays. When it's finished, press the Xbox button to go to the Home screen, or simply wait for it to appear. Congratulations, you are now at the Home screen and ready to enjoy your new Xbox One!

MORE ON MICROSOFT ACCOUNTS

Although you can use an existing third-party email address to set up an official Microsoft account, Microsoft obviously prefers that you set one up using one of its own web-based services, such as Outlook.com. Believe it or not, we think this is a good idea, too.

That said, we suggest you take this a step further and use your Microsoft account only for Xbox login and for logging in to Windows 8–based systems. Give it a password you don't use anywhere else, and don't use it for email, especially when creating login accounts at other websites. Over time, your Microsoft account accumulates a lot of information, including what credit card you use if you choose to make purchases through the Microsoft Store, so following this advice helps keep that information even more secure.

Playing Discs

Your Xbox One can play game discs licensed by Microsoft specifically for this platform (see Chapter 5, "Getting Your Game On," for additional information); region 1 DVDs, which are sold in the United States, Canada, Bermuda, and U.S. territories, and region A/1 Blu-rays, which include most of the Americas, as well as many East Asian and Southeast Asian territories (see "Playing DVDs and Blu-rays" in Chapter 7, "Viewing Videos and Video Content," for additional information); and any CD music/audio discs (see "Streaming Your Personal Music Library" in Chapter 8, "Tuning In to Music," for additional information).

Xbox One–compatible retail games are easily identified by the prominence of the Xbox One logo, green case, and gray accented spine

Saving Your Discs!

Never move your Xbox One with a disc inside, because there is a risk of the disc getting scratched by the console's optical drive, rendering the disc unusable and possibly damaging the inside of your console.

Insert and Remove Discs

When handling your discs, try not to touch the unlabeled side. A disc should always be grasped by its outer edges or center hole area.

Insert the disc in the disc slot with the label side up until you start to feel a slight resistance. The Xbox One automatically pulls in the disc the rest of the way.

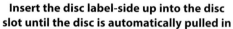

Insert the disc label-side up into the disc slot until the disc is automatically pulled in

If it's a game, the disc either begins installing onto the hard drive if this is the first time the game is being used, or begins playing if it was previously installed onto the hard drive. If it's a video or music disc, the disc either begins installing the appropriate app if this is the first time you're using a particular format, or, if the app was previously installed, it begins playing.

If you want to eject a disc, press the Eject button on the front of the console.

Warning

You can eject a disc at any time, but you might lose unsaved data. Try to quit whatever related activity you're doing before ejecting a disc.

Although your Xbox is a well-built piece of electronic equipment, you might at some point find yourself with an eject command that doesn't function properly. This can be especially disconcerting if your favorite game or movie is stuck in there, but don't fret. It's possible to reclaim your disc. All you need to accomplish this feat is a straightened paper clip.

Manually Eject Discs

If your disc gets stuck, disconnect your console from the power cord and any other cables, and then follow these steps to reclaim it from your console:

1. Locate the yellow sticker behind the ventilation vents on the left side of the console.

2. Insert the straight end of a paper clip into the eject hole, which is next to the yellow sticker.

3. When the disc pops out slightly, use your fingers to pull the disc out the rest of the way. At this point, you can reconnect your console.

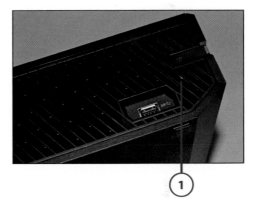

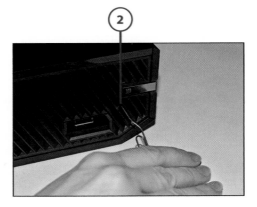

Check It Out

After you remove the stuck disc, be sure to check whether it's undamaged, with its label intact and no stickiness present. If the disc is damaged in any way, do not place it back into your Xbox One. Instead, seek a replacement.

Setting Up a Cable or Satellite Connection

When your cable or satellite receiver box is connected to the HDMI input on your Xbox One, there are only three additional prerequisites for getting the most out of your TV-viewing experience. First, as with most Xbox One features, you need an active Xbox Live Gold membership (see Chapter 3). Second, you need an active Internet connection to download channel lineup information for the OneGuide, which is how you control and select TV from your Xbox (see "Working with OneGuide" in Chapter 7). Finally, you need to make sure Kinect is plugged in and active to send infrared (IR) commands to your television and cable or satellite receiver box.

It's Not All Good

Not all cable or satellite receiver boxes are set to receive infrared commands. Instead, they might use radio frequency (RF) or other control technologies. Check the manual that came with your cable or satellite receiver box to see how to enable Infrared mode. Otherwise, you can skip television control setup and exclusively use the remote control that came with your cable or satellite receiver box.

Begin First-Time Setup

To begin first-time TV setup, follow these steps:

1. Select the TV tile. If it's not on the Home screen, find it under My Games & Apps.

2. Select Start.

3. When the Xbox One detects a signal from your cable or satellite receiver box, select Next.

4. Select Set It Up if you want to use your voice to turn on and adjust the volume of your TV, then proceed to the next step. If not, skip to step 13.

A new way to watch TV

- Don't miss a thing. Watch TV alongside your games.
- "Xbox on." Control your entertainment system through your Xbox.
- No more remotes! Change channels with your voice.

② Start

Back

Skip

Let's watch TV

We've detected a signal from your cable or satellite box.

It may take up to 12 seconds for your picture to show up here. When it does, select Next.

③ Next

Back

Turn on your TV when you say "Xbox on"

You can use your voice to turn on and adjust the volume of your TV. We'll need to know a few things about your TV first.

If you have an audio receiver, you can set it up later in Settings > TV & OneGuide.

④ Set it up

Back

Skip

5. Select the brand of your television. If you don't see your brand in the drop-down list, select I Don't See My Brand and enter the brand manually.

6. Select Next.

7. Select Send Command to send the Mute command to your TV. This should mute your TV.

8. If the Mute command worked, select Yes. Otherwise, select No to try again. If you're not sure, select I'm Not Sure, Try Again, which will send the same command.

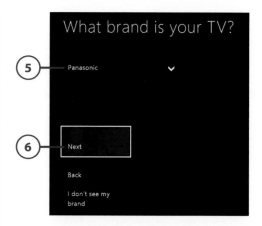

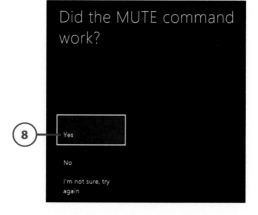

9. Select Send Command to test whether the Info/Display command works.

10. If the Info/Display command worked, select Yes; otherwise, select No to try again. If you're not sure, select I'm Not Sure, Try Again, which will send the same command.

11. Select Send Command to test whether the Menu command works.

Ready to send the INFO/DISPLAY command to your TV...

Close any TV menus. We'll send a command to your TV to see if it works.

⑨ Send command

Back

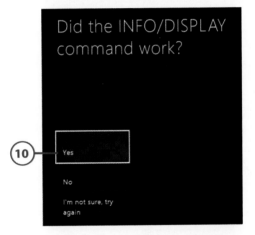

Did the INFO/DISPLAY command work?

⑩ Yes

No

I'm not sure, try again

Ready to send the MENU command to your TV...

Close any TV menus. We'll send a command to your TV to see if it works.

⑪ Send command

Back

12. If the Menu command worked, select Yes; otherwise, select No to try again. If you're not sure, select I'm Not Sure, Try Again, which will send the same command.

Trouble with IR

For troubleshooting issues about sending IR commands, refer to https://support.xbox.com/en-US/xbox-one/live-tv/troubleshoot-oneguide.

13. Select Set Up OneGuide to access TV listings for your cable or satellite system.

14. Enter your ZIP code.

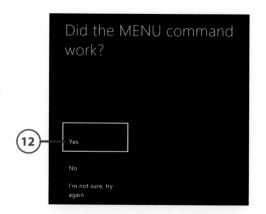

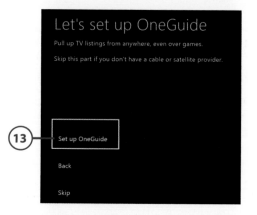

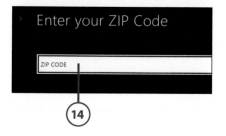

15. Select your TV provider.

16. Select Next.

TV Provider Not Listed?

If your TV provider is not listed, it might not yet be compatible with Xbox One. Refer to http://forums.xbox.com/ xbox_forums/xbox_support/ tv_hardware/default.aspx for more information on possible workarounds or solutions.

17. Select your TV lineup.

18. Select Next.

19. Enter the brand of your cable or satellite receiver box.

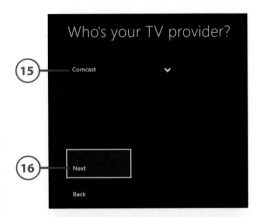

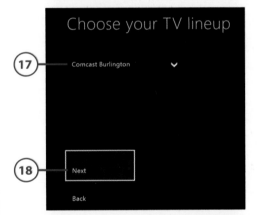

20. Close any menus on your cable or satellite receiver box with your cable or satellite remote. Select Send Command.

21. If the Channel Up command worked, select Yes; otherwise, select No to try again. If you're not sure, select I'm Not Sure, Try Again, which will send the same command.

22. Select Yes if you want Microsoft to track the TV shows you watch so it can improve its TV program and movie recommendations. If not, select No.

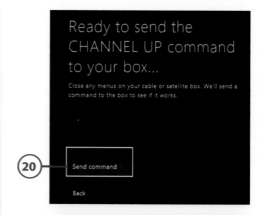

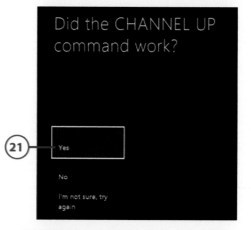

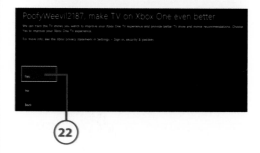

23. Select Next.

24. Select Watch TV.

25. Your television is now full screen. Press the Xbox button on your controller to return to the Home screen.

Your cable or satellite receiver box is now configured to work with your Xbox One and Kinect. See "Working with OneGuide" in Chapter 7 for how to use the OneGuide. See "Display & Sound" in Chapter 2 if you need to set up control of an audio receiver (sound system).

Connecting Additional Controllers

Unless you're perfectly content playing solo offline, you'll want to add additional controllers to your console, or have the ability to connect your friends' controllers to your console; up to eight controllers can be used, though most games don't support that many players. There are three different ways to connect an additional controller or controller paired with a different console to your Xbox One: using Kinect (quickest), using the console's Accessory Pairing button, or using an optional Micro-USB cable or Xbox One Play & Charge Kit.

Use Kinect

To use Kinect to connect a new controller, make sure your console is turned on and that the controller has battery power. Follow these steps:

1. Turn on your controller by pressing and holding the Xbox button until the controller turns on. The Xbox button pulses, indicating it is not yet paired.

2. Press and release the Connect button on the controller. The controller's Xbox button flashes a few times as it searches for the console.

3. From anywhere in the room, point the front of the controller toward the Kinect. Once connected, the Xbox button lights solid white. Repeat this procedure for any additional controllers you would like to connect.

Use the Accessory Pairing Button

After turning on your Xbox One console and making sure the controller has power, follow these steps to connect another controller using the console's Accessory Pairing button:

1. Turn on your controller by pressing and holding the Xbox button until the controller turns on. The Xbox button pulses, indicating it is not yet paired.

2. Press and release the Accessory Pairing button on the side of the console.

3. Press and release the Connect button on the controller. This must be done within 20 seconds of step 2. The controller's Xbox button flashes a few times as it searches for the console. When it's connected, the Xbox button lights solid white. Repeat this procedure for any additional controllers you would like to connect.

Use a Micro-USB Cable

To pair a controller with the Xbox One over USB, simply connect a Micro-USB cable, which is the same type of cable that comes with the Xbox One Play & Charge Kit (see "Accessorizing Your Xbox One" in Chapter 4) and many mobile devices, to both the controller and an available USB port on the console. The controller is now paired with the console.

Plug in this end to one of the console's USB ports

Plug in this end to the controller's USB charge port

If no batteries or battery pack are installed in the controller, it will now function as a wired controller. If the controller has working AA batteries installed, or a rechargeable battery pack with a sufficient charge, the controller can now be unplugged from the newly paired console and used normally.

Setting Up Your Headset

The included Xbox One chat headset works great for party chat (see Chapter 6, "Making the Social Connection") and intense, smack-talking online gaming sessions. It's also easy to connect. Follow these steps:

1. Insert the expansion port connector on the headset into the bottom of the controller until it slides securely in place.

2. Adjust the height of the earpiece by sliding it up or down until it is comfortable.

3. Swivel the microphone so that the end is close to your mouth.

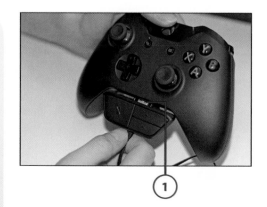

Understanding Your Warranty

The warranty period on your Xbox One console and Kinect is 1 year, and for other accessories is 90 days. During this time, you can return the console, Kinect, or other accessories to Microsoft for servicing free of charge, provided troubleshooting does not resolve your problem. However, before any service can be performed, you must register your console at https://myservice.xbox.com/. The same Microsoft account used to sign in to Xbox Live is required for registration, as well as your console or Kinect's serial number.

To send your Xbox One, Kinect, or accessories to Microsoft for servicing after registration, visit http://www.support.xbox.com (U.S. residents only). Alternatively, you can call (800) 4MY-XBOX.

Extending Your Warranty

One way to extend your warranty is by purchasing Microsoft Complete after registration. As of this writing, extending your console's and Kinect's warranty to 3 years costs $69.99.

Servicing costs vary, but you can generally get a slightly reduced rate if you submit your request online rather than over the phone. Turnaround time on repairs varies by your state, but generally ranges between 12 and 19 days. When your console, Kinect, or accessories are no longer under warranty, you can still send them to Microsoft for servicing if any problems arise.

**Learn about the Home
screen and how to
navigate it**

**Discover how to
multitask with Snap**

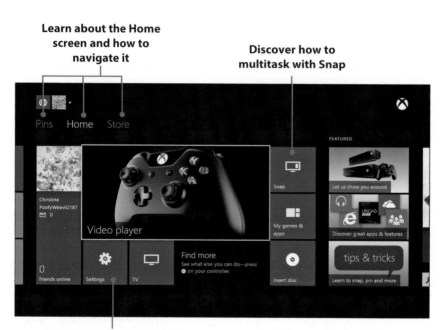

**Become familiar with your
Xbox One's Settings**

In this chapter, you learn how to navigate your Xbox One console and become familiar with its Dashboard and settings.

→ Navigating the Dashboard with Your Controller
→ Understanding the Dashboard Content
→ Understanding Kinect Controls
→ Breaking Down the Settings Screen
→ Changing the Console Settings
→ Adjusting Family Settings
→ Managing Other People and Guest Settings
→ Multitasking with Snap

Navigating Your Xbox One's Dashboard and Settings

To fully enjoy your Xbox One's rich gaming and multimedia capabilities, you need to become familiar with its Dashboard and settings and learn how to navigate your console. Xbox One enables you to control the system, its Dashboard, and the devices to which it's connected by using the controller, motion, or voice controls through Kinect, or a combination of these.

In this chapter, you become familiar with the Xbox One Dashboard and learn how to navigate it in all the aforementioned ways. You also learn how to adjust your console's settings to suit your needs, pin and unpin apps, navigate the Store, and discover how to multitask using Snap.

Navigating the Dashboard with Your Controller

It's best to get a lay of the rich Xbox One landscape using a reliable navigation vehicle, and the controller is by far the easiest way to get around. Unlike Kinect's voice and motion controls, which are discussed later in this chapter, it's never fussy and is, in fact, quite intuitive.

If you need a refresher on the components of your Xbox One controller before proceeding to the general navigation rules, see the Prologue, "Getting to Know the Xbox One." Otherwise, this is how you'll navigate the Xbox One Dashboard using your controller:

- **Moving left, right, up, and down**—Use the left stick or the D-pad. To more quickly move left and right (but not up and down), you can also use the left bumper and right bumper, respectively.

- **Selecting items**—Press the A button when the item is highlighted (outlined in white).

- **Going back or exiting an app or screen**—Press the B button.

- **Going back to the default Home screen**—Press the Xbox button.

- **Opening app-related menus**—Press the Menu button.

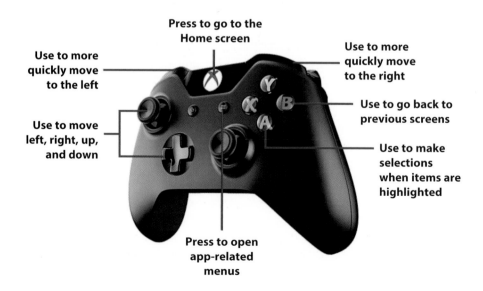

Press to go to the Home screen

Use to more quickly move to the left

Use to more quickly move to the right

Use to go back to previous screens

Use to move left, right, up, and down

Use to make selections when items are highlighted

Press to open app-related menus

Understanding the Dashboard Content

The Xbox One Dashboard consists of three distinct areas that contain a variety of tiles that divide content, settings, and functions into specific categories, similar to the user experience provided by Windows 8 and vaguely reminiscent of the Xbox 360 interface. These areas include Home, Pins, and Store, with the latter two being an extension of the Home screen. There is also a Quick Info area that appears at the very top of each of the Home screens. In this area, you'll encounter several thumbnail-sized tiles, including a Notification and Gamertag tile.

All features of your Xbox One Dashboard are available when you're logged in to Xbox Live. If you don't have an Xbox Live account, fewer options are accessible. For more on Xbox Live, turn to Chapter 3, "Examining Xbox Live."

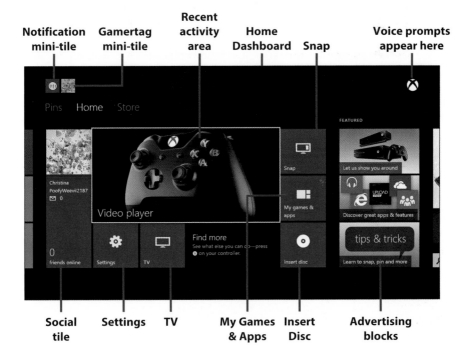

Reviewing the Home Screen

The Home screen is the default view. Although you can't customize this screen manually, as you can with many Windows applications, it becomes tailored based on how you use your Xbox One.

These are the items you'll encounter on your virgin Dashboard:

- **Notification mini-tile**—Part of the Quick Info area, this option enables you to access any notifications, including for Skype, messaging, and parties, among others. You have the opportunity to tailor the notifications you receive here by selecting the Preferences option from the Settings menu, which is discussed in greater detail in the "Changing the Console Settings" section later in this chapter.

- **Gamertag mini-tile**—Another option in the Quick Info area, this item shows you which player is signed in to the console. In addition, by selecting this tile, you can sign in other people to your console.

- **Social tile**—This tile provides at-a-glance information related to you, whether you have any messages, and how many of your friends are online. Upon selecting this tile, you can access your profile, friends, followers, and messages. You can also add people and find additional connections. Turn to Chapter 4, "Personalizing Your Xbox One Experience," for information on how to adjust your profile and customize your Xbox One experience.

- **Recent activity area**—This is the largest block and appears front and center. What is shown in this area changes based on your most recent activity, enabling you to get back into that activity quickly, if desired.

- **Settings**—Selecting this option is your portal into your Xbox One settings, which dictate your user experience. You'll find options that are specific to your personal Xbox account, those that address your general console settings, and those that enable you to manage settings for other individuals who use your console. You'll learn more details about the settings in the "Breaking Down the Settings Screen" section later in this chapter.

Accessing Settings via Your Controller

You can access the settings any time with your controller. Just go to the Home screen and press the Menu button on your controller.

- **TV**—This option enables you to set up your TV to work in collaboration with your console, letting you control your TV through your console, change channels using only your voice, and watch TV while gaming.

Once this is set up, you'll be able to use it to access your TV. For details on how to set up your TV, turn to "Setting Up a Cable or Satellite Connection" in Chapter 1, "Setting Up Your Xbox One."

- **Snap**—This application enables you to multitask by letting you run two applications simultaneously. While you're engaged in your primary activity, you can dock another app on the right side of the screen. For more on Snap, turn to the "Multitasking with Snap" section later in this chapter.

- **My Games & Apps**—This option is your portal to all of your gaming-related activities, providing access to your avatar, friends, messages, and settings. You can also access Internet Explorer, the Xbox One Store, among other options.

- **Insert Disc**—This indicates what disc is in your Xbox One console at any given time. When no disc is inserted, it just says Insert Disc.

- **Featured blocks**—These are advertising blocks that change based on what Microsoft wants to showcase. They are in no way obtrusive or irritating…except that yes, yes they really are.

Examining Pins

To the far left of the main Home screen is the Pins area. You can manually customize this area by pinning your favorite games, apps, or web pages, enabling you to quickly locate the media that you use and interact with most frequently. Think of the pins you set as bookmarks.

Even before you manually pin any content to this section, it contains the following items, which you can unpin (remove) at any time:

- **OneDrive**—Enables you to store your photo and video files in the cloud so that you can view them from your TV. In addition, you can use it to play slideshows and view photos and videos that others share with you. For more on OneDrive, turn to Chapter 9, "Managing Files with OneDrive."

- **Skype**—Enables you to enjoy free and unlimited voice and HD video calls with anyone else on Skype. For more on Skype, turn to "Keeping in Touch via Skype" in Chapter 6, "Making the Social Connection."

- **TV**—Provides the same portal as initially appears on the main Home screen. For more on getting your TV to work in unity with your Xbox One, turn to "Setting Up a Cable or Satellite Connection" in Chapter 1.

- **Xbox Music**—Enables you to listen to live streaming music on your Xbox One. However, this streaming music service is an application you must pay for to maximize the use of this service. For more on Xbox Music, turn to Chapter 8, "Tuning In to Music."

- **Xbox Video**—Enables you to rent and buy movies and watch TV shows. You can also use it to stream your personal videos to Xbox One from compatible Windows tablets and computers. To learn more about this app, see "Enjoying TV Shows, Music Videos, and Movies with Xbox Video" in Chapter 7.

Pinning content to the Home screen enables you to easily access your favorite stuff, much like bookmarks help you find pages in a book. You can pin anything from favorite apps and games to web pages, and they'll then appear under the Pins section of the Home screen.

Pin and Unpin Content

Follow these steps to pin/unpin content using your controller, which is by far the easiest way to accomplish these tasks:

1. Go to the Home screen. If you're in an application, you can easily get to the Home screen by pressing the Xbox button on your controller.

2. Move to an area of the screen where you can access the game, music, video, or app you want to pin so that it becomes highlighted (outlined in white) on the Xbox One Dashboard. Press the A button to select it.

3. Scroll to the specific item that you want to pin so that it is highlighted, and press the Menu button.

4. From the menu that appears, select the Pin to Home option. Your item is now pinned.

5. To unpin an item, highlight it in the Pins area of your Dashboard, select the Menu button once again, and this time select the Unpin option. Your item is now unpinned from the Home screen.

Checking Out the Store

To the far right of the main Home screen is the Store. Here, you can peruse and purchase a variety of content from the Xbox One Store, which features Games, Movies & TV, Music, and Apps departments. Occasionally, heavily discounted or even free items are made available for download, so it's worth checking out the Store from time to time.

Here's what each department has in store (pun intended) for you:

- **Games**—You can find games through a variety of means. You can peruse games that are being highlighted, which are broken down into various Popular Games categories, including Featured, New Releases, Top Games Right Now, Recommended for You, New Game Demos, Top Selling, and Top Rated. You can also search for games by selecting the Search Games tile and redeem game-related goods using a code by selecting the Use a Code tile. For more on gaming on your console and games to consider, turn to Chapter 5, "Getting Your Game On."

- **Movies & TV**—From this option, you can browse and access movies and TV shows, which are organized into a variety of categories, includ- ing Featured Movies, Featured TV Shows, New Movies, New TV Shows, Top Rented Movies, Movies Recommended for You, TV Shows Recom- mended for You, Top Selling TV Shows, Top Rated Movies, and Top Rated TV Shows. You can also search for video-related content by selecting the Search Videos tile, as well as access the Xbox Video app. For more on viewing videos and video content on your console, turn to Chapter 7.

- **Music**—The Music section has only a Featured category. You can also search for music by selecting the Search Music tile and access the Xbox Music app. For more on enjoying music on your Xbox One, turn to Chapter 8.

- **Apps**—In this department, the available apps are categorized into Featured, Popular Apps, and New Releases. You can find apps by selecting the Search Apps tile and use a code to redeem an app by selecting the Use a Code tile. Turn to "Using Apps to Watch Video" in Chapter 7 for some video-related apps that are worth checking out.

Understanding Kinect Controls

After setting up the Kinect sensor as described in "Power on for the First Time" in Chapter 1, you can use your Kinect to navigate your Xbox One. You can do this using motion gestures or your voice. Although both of these options work quite well, particularly when you understand how to use them, they don't always work as flawlessly as using your controller. Of course, as the system matures and updates refine and add to existing features, the sensitivity of both motion and voice controls is likely to improve considerably.

The following section shows you how to use motions and voice to control your Xbox. When outlining how to perform tasks throughout the remainder of this book, the text mainly focuses on using the controller because there is far less room for user error or technical issues arising, and you don't want to read a 700-page manual, do you? Still, you can apply the information you learn here to other tasks.

As you interact with your Xbox One, practice both motion and voice controls. Doing so will help you become one with your system—after all, you'll become a living controller. And the voice controls do, in fact, make some tasks much simpler than reaching for a controller. In addition, having these extra navigation/control options at your disposal can make it easier for you to accomplish tasks.

Navigating the Dashboard via Motion Controls

You can use six specific motions to control your Xbox One console. These are for returning Home, making a selection, scrolling through a screen, opening the system menu, opening onscreen notifications, and zooming in and out. Although many of these tasks use fairly intuitive motions, you must remember the sequences to perform them properly and execute the desired task. Therefore, take some time to practice them, particularly if you want to employ this mode of navigation on a regular basis.

Before you can initiate any of these motion controls, you must engage your Kinect by lifting your hand up and then putting it down again.

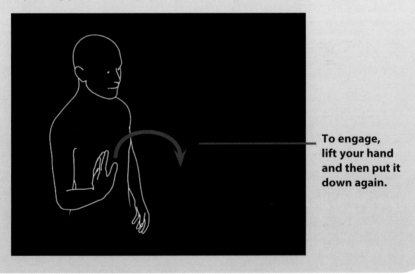

To engage, lift your hand and then put it down again.

Return Home

To return Home using motion controls, follow these steps:

1. Hold out both of your hands toward the edge of the screen, making sure your hands are open and your palms are facing inward.

2. As you close your hands, move them toward each other in front of your chest. You're now at the Home screen.

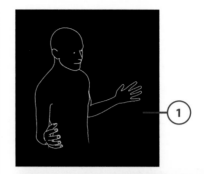

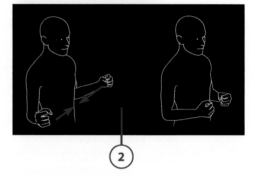

Select Items

To select items, follow these steps:

1. Raise one of your hands so that an open palm faces the sensor.

2. Move your hand so that it rests over the tile/item you want, and push your hand forward.

3. Now pull your hand back toward your body to make the selection.

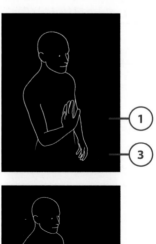

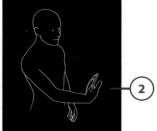

Scroll Through a Screen

To scroll through screens, follow these steps:

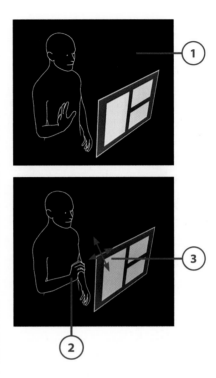

1. Raise one of your hands so that an open palm faces the sensor.

2. When the hand icon appears, close your hand anywhere over the area you want to scroll.

3. Move your hand left or right to pull the screen in the desired direction. You can also move your hand up or down to go in these directions if an app you're in supports vertical scrolling.

Open App-Specific System Menus

In addition to being able to open full apps, you can open app-specific system menus. To do so, follow these steps:

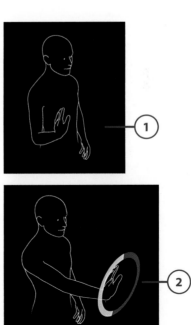

1. Raise one of your hands so that an open palm faces the sensor.

2. Push your arm forward toward the Kinect and hold it steady until a circle timer appears. When the ring comes full circle, a system menu appears from which you can select the item you want.

Open Onscreen Notifications

When you see you have an onscreen notification, you can open it as follows:

1. Hold both hands in front of you and move them together in front of your chest.

2. Grip with both hands.

3. Pull apart, moving both hands out horizontally.

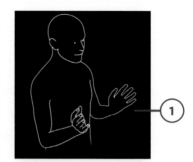

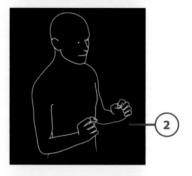

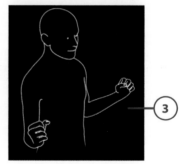

Zoom In and Out

To zoom in and out, follow these steps:

1. Raise one of your hands so that an open palm faces the sensor.

2. When the hand icon appears onscreen, close your hand over the area you want to zoom into or out of.

3. Pull your hand toward you to zoom in. To zoom out again, push your hand away from your body and toward the screen.

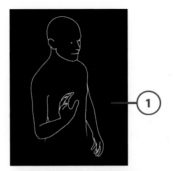

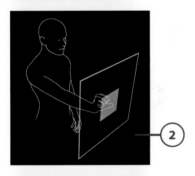

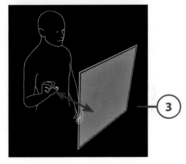

>>>Go Further

VIEWING THE GESTURES VIDEO TUTORIAL ONLINE

Sometimes, written instructions can leave you feeling a bit confused, even when photographs accompany them. If you find this to be the case, check out the Gesture Tutorial in the Help app on your console. To get to the Help app, go to the Home screen, press the Menu button on your controller, select Help, and then select How-To Videos & Tutorials. Keep in mind that you might have to scroll to another page to find the information you seek, as things are bound to move around. We urge you to give the tutorial a try. It's like a fun little mini-game.

Navigating the Dashboard via Voice Controls

Although Kinect generally does a good job of picking up voice commands, it might not always work flawlessly. Kinect seems to have some difficulty deciphering certain voices and accents, so there might be times when you need to repeat commands. Similarly, it's very good at executing some commands ("Xbox, pause"), whereas it really struggles with others, like when you tell it to tune to a specific TV station. Again, as the system evolves, this is likely to become much less of a problem.

Nevertheless, you can take several actions to improve the odds of Kinect understanding your voice commands:

- **Minimizing background noise**—Try to minimize as much background noise as possible. If you're blasting music or someone is running the vacuum, for example, your Kinect might not be able to hear your voice among the auditory clutter.

- **Ensuring Kinect is properly located and calibrated**—Make sure your Kinect sensor is positioned so that it can hear and recognize your voice commands. (See "Making a Home for Your Xbox One" in Chapter 1.) In addition, your Kinect must be calibrated for it to function properly. For more on this, see the "Kinect" section later in this chapter.

- **Speaking normally but clearly**—When making voice commands, use your normal speaking voice and speech pattern, but be sure to speak clearly. You don't want to slur your words or yell at Kinect, which can make it difficult for the sensor to decipher your prompts. But if you tend to speak more quietly or have a softer voice, you might need to project your voice a bit. And one last comment, if your house is bilingual or you have a guest over who speaks a different language, Kinect might not understand your voice commands if multiple languages are being spoken, especially if an individual in focus is speaking a different language than you are.

- **Pausing before saying each command**—Most Xbox voice commands start with the word "Xbox." Make sure you pause a second after saying "Xbox" and before you proceed with the voice shortcut that follows, such as "go Home." If you say the command too quickly, your Kinect sensor might not recognize that you're directing commands at it. However, when you become familiar with using voice commands and know the voice shortcuts, you can reduce this extended pause time.

Table 2.1 outlines the voice shortcuts you can use. Don't worry about memorizing them. You can always say "Xbox, select" to see the commands available to you. Also, whenever any text appears in green, it can be spoken as a command.

Table 2.1 Kinect Voice Shortcuts for Controlling Your Xbox One Console

Spoken Command	Resulting Action
General Prompts	
"Xbox, on"	Wakes up your Xbox One, turning on your TV and cable/satellite set-top box
"Xbox, turn off"	Puts Xbox One to sleep and/or turns it off, which might include turning off your TV and cable/satellite set-top box
"Xbox"	Shows a menu of global voice shortcuts; if you say "More shortcuts," the full list appears
"Xbox, select"	Shows voice commands on the screen; any green text can be spoken
"Stop listening"	Stops Kinect from using voice commands on the screen in that moment
"Xbox, help"	Shows help for the app you're currently in
"Xbox, use a code"	Initiates Kinect code for scanning QR codes*
"Xbox, show notification"	Opens the notification center and shows your most recent notification

Spoken Command	Resulting Action
Identity Prompts	
"Xbox, sign in"	Signs you in
"Xbox, sign in as [name a particular Xbox Live user here]"	Sign in another Xbox Live user
"Xbox, sign out"	Signs you out
"Xbox, sign out as [name a particular Xbox Live user here]"	Signs out another Xbox Live user
Gaming Prompts	
"Xbox, record that"	Records the previous 30 seconds of gameplay
"Xbox, invite"	Launches the Party app in Snap mode
Volume Controls	
"Xbox, volume up"	Turns volume of TV set up
"Xbox, volume down"	Turns volume of TV set down
"Xbox, mute"	Mutes sound on your TV
"Xbox, unmute"	Unmutes sound on your TV
Dashboard Navigation and Multitasking Prompts	
"Xbox, go Home" or "Xbox, show my stuff"	Returns to Home
"Xbox, go to [name a particular game or app here]"	Launches your desired game or app, provided it's installed on your system
"Xbox, show menu"	Opens the menu for the game or app you're in; this is the equivalent of pressing the Menu button on your controller
"Xbox, go back"	Returns to the previous screen
"Xbox, Snap [name a particular app here]"	Launches app in Snap mode
"Xbox, unsnap"	Unsnaps app from Snap mode
"Xbox, switch"	Switches the focus between the two apps on the screen
"Xbox, Bing"	Launches Bing, enabling you to search for games, music, movies, and TV shows

Spoken Command	Resulting Action
Communication Prompts	
"Xbox, Skype [name person here]"	Pulls up details for the person, provided he or she is a contact in your Skype favorites list on your Xbox One
"Xbox, call [name person here]"	Initiates a video call with the desired individual, provided he or she is a contact in your Skype favorites list on your Xbox One
"Xbox, answer"	Answers any incoming Skype call with video chat
"Xbox, answer without video"	Answers any incoming Skype call so that the caller only hears your voice
"Xbox, hang up"	Ends Skype call
"Xbox, send a message"	Enables you to send a message to your Xbox Live friends
TV-Related Prompts	
"Xbox, watch TV"	Launches cable/satellite TV from your set-top box
"Xbox, watch [say name of channel here]"	Changes cable/satellite TV to the desired channel; if you are in the Xbox OneGuide, any program/channel shown in green can be spoken
"Xbox, show guide" or "Xbox, OneGuide"	Launches the Xbox OneGuide, which outlines your available TV programming provided your cable/satellite company is a participant
Media Prompts (Transport Controls)	
"Xbox play," "Xbox stop," "Xbox pause," "Xbox fast forward," "Xbox rewind," "Xbox faster," "Xbox slower," "Xbox skip forward," "Xbox skip backward," "Xbox next song," and "Xbox previous song"	Transports controls for media playback are all self-explanatory, and they also work during gameplay
"Xbox, play music"	Resumes playing the most recent song in Xbox Music

QR codes are a type of square bar code that is optically readable, including by your Kinect sensor. They are intended to make your Xbox One entertainment experience more pleasurable. For example, if you have an Xbox Store gift card, you can hold the QR code up to Kinect and redeem it instantly, saving you time from entering long codes into your system.

It's Not All Good

Trouble Getting Kinect to Turn Your Console On or Off

With so much sensitive hardware and software to contend with, things can go wrong at times with your Xbox One console, such as Kinect being unable to turn your console on or off using voice commands or recognizing your prompts. If this happens to you, don't fret! In addition to the recommended actions to improve the odds of Kinect understanding your voice commands, you can try these troubleshooting strategies:

- **Check your Kinect sensor**—Your Kinect sensor must be plugged into your Xbox One console and enabled in the Settings menu for it to work. To verify that your sensor is enabled, press the Menu button on your controller, select Settings, and then select Kinect. Make sure that your Kinect sensor is plugged into your console and that the sensor turns on when your console is on. If it doesn't turn on, unplug it for about 10 seconds, and then plug it back in.

- **Ensure there is power**—Is the LED indicator light on your power brick glowing white or orange? If not, you do not have power. Check that your power supply is firmly plugged into the wall outlet and into your Xbox One console.

- **Restart your Xbox One console**—If you unplugged your Kinect sensor or experienced a power outage, the sensor might not be listening for voice commands. By powering your console all the way down (shut it down, unplug it, and then plug it back in), you can reengage Kinect so that it listens to you.

Breaking Down the Settings Screen

When you select the Settings tile from the Home screen, a variety of options become available to you. To the far left, you'll find access to a variety of options that are specific to your personal Xbox account. The middle section includes tiles for all of your console's settings, which are discussed in greater detail in the "Changing the Console Settings" section later in this chapter. To the far right, you can add, remove, and tweak settings of family members and others using your Xbox One console. You also can access a Guest Settings tile, which enables you to create a guest key. These options are outlined in greater detail later in this chapter.

What follows is a brief description of the Settings options on the far left, many of which are outlined in other chapters or later in this chapter:

- **About Me**—Here, you can adjust the information tied to your profile, including your gamerpic, gamertag, avatar, and privacy settings. For more on what you can do here, turn to Chapter 4.

- **Sign-in, Security & Passkey**—Here, you can create a passkey, which is a protective six-digit code; tweak your Kinect and console sign-in settings; and access a variety of legal documents. See "Set Up a Passkey" later in this section.

- **Privacy & Online Safety**—This area enables you to set a variety of privacy defaults, selecting from child, teen, and adult defaults, or creating your own custom defaults (see Table 2.2 for what these mean, so you can decide accordingly). You also can adjust your content restrictions, such as whether you want any explicit text blocked, and select your contact preferences, including whether you'd like to receive offers from Xbox and companies providing Xbox-compatible products.

- **Payment & Billing**—Here, you can add credit card and billing information to your account.

- **Subscriptions**—This is where you manage your Xbox Live Gold membership, Xbox Music Pass account, and other paid subscriptions. Turn to Chapter 3 for more on Xbox Live and to Chapter 8 for details about Xbox Music and the Music Pass.

- **My Home Xbox**—From this area, people can play games downloaded to your console without having to sign in as you. It extends Xbox Live Gold membership to your entire household.

Table 2.2   Decoding Your Xbox One's Default Privacy and Online Safety Settings

Setting	Description
Adult default	This provides the most social experience, enabling the following: • Everyone can see your friends, game clips, online status, availability to play, and which music, apps, and games you've enjoyed. • Your friends can see your profile and any details you add, such as your bio and motto. • Microsoft can use your video app history to customize your experiences. • Microsoft can store any exercise information with your online profile; however, this information is kept private.
Teen default	This places moderate controls so that users are shielded against certain experiences: • Only friends can see your online status, profile, friends' list, game clips, and any music, apps, and games you've enjoyed. • You can play and download free games, music, videos, and apps; make game clips; and see Kinect content other people create. • You can add friends and view other people's profiles and their friends. • You can socialize in parties and multiplayer games, share Kinect content you create, communicate with friends, and share experiences on social networks. • The same Microsoft capabilities as for Adult defaults are in force here.
Child default	This establishes more privacy than the other defaults, enabling the following: • Users can play and download free games, music, videos, and apps, and they can make game clips of their best moments. • Users can see other people's profiles and created content, but need a parent to add friends. • Only the users' friends can communicate with them and see when they're online and available to play. • The same Microsoft capabilities as for Adult defaults are in force here.

Setting	Description
Custom	Selecting this option enables you to tailor your (or another user's) experience, providing the following options for customization:

Your Ability

- Type of content you can buy/download
- Ability to join in multiplayer games on Xbox Live
- Capacity to communicate with others via video
- Ability to add friends
- Capability to view others' Xbox Live profile and created content (does not affect already downloaded content)
- Ability to upload game clips to Xbox Live and broadcast gameplay
- Capacity to share Kinect-created content outside of Xbox Live and to use social networks via Xbox One

Outsider's Ability

- Who can see whether you're online, what you're doing, and whether you're available to play
- Whether others can see the activities you're engaged in at any given time
- Who can communicate with you using voice and texts
- Who can view your Xbox profile, friends' list, game clips, and exercise stats
- Who can view your game and app history, TV/on-demand video history, and music history

Xbox One enables you to tie a six-digit passkey to your profile. This passkey serves several key functions. It prevents children from signing in as their parents and overriding parental controls, yet enables parents to grant content exceptions. It also protects against unauthorized charges, as you can require a passkey to complete transactions on Xbox Live.

When you set a passkey, it roams with you, meaning it follows you to any Xbox One console you use. So if you sign in to your friend's Xbox One console, as long as you sign out when you leave, you can feel secure knowing your account is safely saved to your friend's Xbox One console and ready for you the next time you go over to play.

Set Up a Passkey

To set up a passkey, follow these steps:

1. Go to the Home screen (make sure Home is highlighted/underlined on the Dashboard), press the Menu button on the controller, and select Settings.

2. Select Sign-in, Security & Passkey.

3. Select Create My Passkey.

4. Enter your six-digit passkey.

5. Confirm your passkey.

6. Decide whether sign-in and purchases will require your passkey. When you are finished, press the B button to go back to Settings or the Xbox button to go to the Home screen.

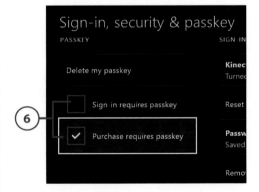

Changing the Console Settings

Your Xbox One enables you to adjust a variety of console settings to suit your needs and preferences, and you don't need to be signed in to your account to do so. You just need to go to the Settings option on the Home screen. Alternatively, you can press the Menu button on your controller and select Settings.

Once in Settings, you can adjust the following console settings:

- **Network**—This is where you tweak your console's capability to connect to Xbox Live, play multiplayer games, and troubleshoot general network performance issues.

- **Kinect**—Go here to turn your Kinect on and off, and to troubleshoot any issues you encounter with your sensor, such as it not recognizing or hearing you.

- **Preferences**—This area enables you to change behaviors on your Xbox One, including notifications, system and app behaviors, and SmartGlass Connections. For more on SmartGlass, turn to Chapter 11, "Looking Through the SmartGlass."

- **TV & OneGuide**—From here, you can troubleshoot TV- and OneGuide-related issues, such as incorrect or missing channel lineups. You also can choose to show only HD or SD channels, or both.

- **Disc & Blu-ray**—This area enables you to adjust disc playback behaviors, including audio, frame rates, and preferred language.

- **System**—Go here to control some of your console's core behaviors, including its name, location/time zone, and system time. You can also restore factory defaults here.

- **Display & Sound**—This is where you adjust your console's display and sound settings by selecting your TV's resolution/connection, color depth, and color space.

- **Closed Captioning**—Go here to turn closed captioning on or off and customize the way captions appear.

- **Power & Startup**—This area enables you to customize the power settings on your Xbox One console, such as by setting it to shut down automatically or having it turn on with a voice command.

Network

When you select Network, you access the Network Settings screen, which is divided into three columns. The left column provides options for setting up a new connection or modifying the existing connection for your home networking devices. The middle column is purely informational, displaying the current status of your network connection (if any connection issues are detected, they'll be outlined here) and the Network Address Translation (NAT) type. Finally, the right column offers options for testing your network connection and troubleshooting network performance issues.

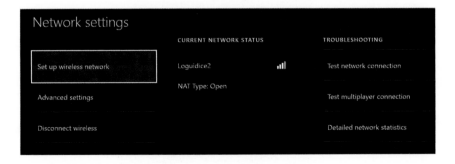

Here's what you need to know about the Network Settings in the left column:

- **Set Up Wireless Network**—Select this option if your Xbox One isn't currently connected to the Internet or if you want to change wireless access points, such as if you've taken your Xbox One to a friend's house.

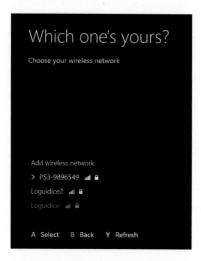

- **Advanced Settings**—Unless you're an advanced user, you can largely ignore this area, which is generally reserved for technical users or support. This is where you can access your Internet Protocol (IP) and Domain Name System (DNS) settings and set up MAC spoofing (changing the Media Access Control [MAC] address of the network interface on your networked device).

- **Disconnect Wireless**—You need to concern yourself with this option only if you're going to be an offline gamer. If so, you still need to connect to Xbox Live on occasion to download the latest system updates. When such updates are completed, you must select the Disconnect Wireless option to get your console offline again. If you were using a wired network connection, you'd only have to disconnect the local area network (LAN) cable from the back of your console to go offline again.

Here's what you need to know about the Current Network Status information in the middle column:

- **Connection indicator**—This indicator tells you whether you're connected and which network you're connected to. If you have a wireless connection, you'll see the signal strength indicator, which can contain one to four bars. One bar indicates a poor signal and four bars indicate an excellent signal.

- **NAT Type**—NAT stands for *Network Address Translation* and it gives you one IP address for internal traffic and another for external traffic, thereby serving as a type of firewall. Don't fret if this means nothing to you. Here's what you need to know: Your NAT type can be Open, Moderate, or Strict. The NAT type determines with whom you can play multiplayer games online and whether you can host matches. An *Open NAT type* enables you to play and host multiplayer games with people who have any NAT type on their network. A *Moderate NAT type* enables you to play multiplayer games with people who have an Open or Moderate NAT type, but you're unlikely to be chosen as the host of a match. A *Strict NAT type* enables you to play multiplayer games only with people who have an Open NAT type, and you can't be chosen to host any matches.

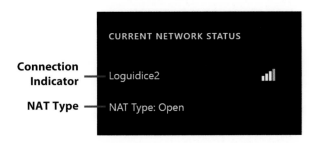

Here's what you need to know about the Troubleshooting options in the right column:

- **Test Network Connection**—Select this option if you can't connect to Xbox Live. It tests your network connection and whether you can connect to the Internet. If a problem is identified, you'll see a summary of where your connection failed and receive troubleshooting steps to help correct the problem. If your connection is good, your console verifies that as well.

- **Test Multiplayer Connection**—Select this option if you experience lag, random disconnects, or other game-related network issues. It tests for anything that could affect your experience while multiplayer gaming on Xbox Live, such as IP address issues and download and upload lags. Your console also verifies whether all is well.

- **Detailed Network Statistics**—This test is intended for networking experts who don't need the troubleshooting guide to correct network performance issues. Selecting this option runs a short test that provides detailed network statistics in a format that's easy to read for those well versed in networking language.

Kinect

When you select Kinect from the Settings screen, you access the Kinect screen, from which you can manage your Kinect. The options are divided into three columns as follows:

- **Kinect**—On the far left, you see whether Kinect is turned on, whether the Kinect microphone is enabled for chat, and what sensor version you have. You also have the option to turn the hand cursor off while watching videos.

- **What Kinect Sees**—In the middle column is a small window showing you exactly what your Kinect sees, including the environment it's capturing and the people in it. If it recognizes any individuals in its field of view, their names and gamerpics appear above them. There is also a What Else Does Kinect See? option. If you select this option, you can see Kinect's field of view in Night mode and infrared. Pressing the A button while this is selected is all that's needed to move through these modes.

Night Mode ──  ── **Infrared**

- **Troubleshooting/Tutorials**—On the right, you see the Troubleshooting area, which provides troubleshooting for both sensor placement/visual field issues and sound detection issues. When you select the I Moved My Kinect Sensor or I'm Having Trouble with Kinect option, you're guided through a series of straightforward calibration tests/options, such as moving your sensor to align a dot with an onscreen series of dots. There is also a handy Tutorials section, from which you can learn all about controlling your Kinect with gestures and voice commands.

Preferences

When you select Preferences from the Settings screen, you access options to tweak your Notifications, System & App preferences, and SmartGlass Connections. If an option is checked off in the Notifications and System & App areas, it means the stated feature is enabled. Under SmartGlass Connections, the option you select appears with a solid circle next to it. For more on SmartGlass, turn to Chapter 11.

Notifications

To the far left are the Notifications options, including for Skype, messages, party invites, and others. You can individually decide which notifications you'd like to receive. When a particular notification is enabled, you'll receive a pop-up whenever such a notification comes through.

When notifications arrive, you can view them by pressing and holding the Xbox button on your controller for a few seconds. Just don't hold it for 5 seconds or longer, as you'll turn off your console and controller. Any notifications you receive remain in the notification center for 1 week, or until you've received more than 50. You can access the notification center by saying "Xbox, show notifications," or by going to the Home screen and choosing the Notification mini-tile.

Keep in mind that some notifications are time-sensitive, such as if you're receiving a party invite. Any commands in these notifications work only if an action is still available, like your friends are still in the party you were invited to. Even if a notification is no longer valid, it won't automatically delete and there is no way to manually delete it.

System & App and SmartGlass Connections

In the middle of the screen is the System & App option and on the right is the SmartGlass Connections option. From these areas, you can change the following preferences:

- **Allow Play To Streaming**—Place a check mark next to this if you want to play video and music on your Xbox One from the Windows 8 and 8.1 Share charm or other Play To compatible devices. Share charm and Play To are applications that make it easy to stream music, video, and photos from your computer to other PCs, TVs, stereos, or devices on your home network.

- **Allow Broadcasts and Game DVR Uploads**—Enable this option if you'd like to use Upload Studio or other broadcast apps, such as Twitch, to capture and share your gameplay footage.

- **Preferred Video Provider**—This feature has not yet been enabled, but in the future you'll be able to pick your preferred video provider here. As of press time, the only option you can select is None.

- **SmartGlass Connections**—SmartGlass enables your Xbox One to interact with your mobile phone, tablet, and other compatible devices, turning these into a second screen to enhance your entertainment experience. You must select what level of SmartGlass capability you'd like enabled.

TV & OneGuide

This is where you go to make changes after you have your TV and OneGuide set up. The initial setup process is outlined in Chapter 1. What follows are the settings you can tweak here:

- **OneGuide**—Select this option to change the programming that shows up in the OneGuide. If you select TV Lineup, you can select your TV provider by entering your ZIP code. If you select Clear OneGuide, you can refresh your OneGuide with the latest Xbox Live information. If you select Clear History, you can clear your personalized viewing history. The final option in this section enables you to choose to show only HD or SD channels, or both.

- **Devices**—Choose this option if you need to set up cable/satellite box, TV, and audio receiver control, or if you'd like to see which devices you currently have connected. You also have the option of removing a cable/satellite box, TV, or audio receiver.

- **Power Settings**—This option enables you to select which devices to turn on and off when you say "Xbox, on" and "Xbox, turn off." You can select from the following options: "Xbox, On" Turns On My Devices, "Xbox, Turn Off" Turns Off My Audio Receiver, "Xbox, Turn Off" Turns Off My Cable or Satellite Box, and "Xbox, Turn Off" Turns Off My TV. Keep in mind that these devices are turned on and off by these prompts along with your Xbox One console.

- **Troubleshooting**—Select this option to set up your TV picture; reset your settings, which clears all TV settings and requires you to set up your TV again when it restarts; or change advanced settings, such as the IR delay (the speed at which commands are sent to your cable/satellite box), remote codes that control the devices hooked up to your console, and audio details.

- **Share My Info with Xbox**—You can decide whether to track the TV shows you watch to improve your TV experience.

- **Done**—Select this option to go back to the main Settings screen.

Disc & Blu-ray

When you select Disc & Blu-ray from the Settings screen, you can set your Xbox One console behavior for disc playback. You'll find three basic types of settings under this option: Disc, Blu-ray, and Preferred Language. These enable the following:

- **Disc**—Here, you'll find two options: Play Disc Automatically and Resume Playback. Check the Play Disc Automatically option if you'd like your discs to begin playing automatically when you insert them. Check the Resume Playback option if you'd like the player to bookmark the point at which you stopped watching your discs so that they resume at the same point when you watch them again.

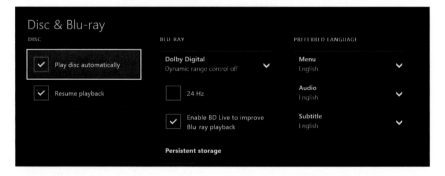

- **Blu-Ray**—There are several advanced settings you can tweak for the Blu-ray player app, which is a separate download (refer to "Playing DVDs and Blu-rays" in Chapter 7). First, there is a Dolby Digital option, which enables you to adjust your system's dynamic range control (this modifies the audio to keep a consistent volume even through the loudest action scenes so that you don't constantly need to turn your volume up and down). If you select Dolby Digital, there are three options: Dynamic Range Control Off, which means this feature is turned off and the intensity of the sound will vary (select this option if you're fine with loudness—this is considered the optimal setting); Dynamic Range Control On, which turns this sound filtering on to keep dialogue and action scenes at a consistent sound level (select this if you don't want to disturb others); and Dynamic Range Control Auto, which lets your system decide based on the material whether this feature should be on or off.

Second, you'll see 24Hz. This is the natural frame rate for movie viewing. If you primarily watch Blu-ray content, you might want to enable it.

Third, you'll see Enable BD Live to Improve Blu-ray Playback. This setting enables access to additional features and content through the BD-Live service. So when you insert a Blu-ray disc, you can connect to the Internet to access this additional media.

Finally, you'll see Persistent Storage. Select this if you want to clear Blu-ray data that has been cached to the console. Sometimes this needs to be cleared so that you can access related content from other discs, but your Xbox One should inform you when you've reached the maximum amount of content that can be held in persistent storage.

- **Preferred Language**—Here, you can select your preferred language for movie menus (Menu), the audio track of your movie (Audio), and subtitles (Subtitle). Keep in mind that these language settings are defaults and might not be supported by all movies.

System

The system settings enable you to learn about and control some of your console's core behaviors.

The options on the far left include

- **Name**—Select this option to name your Xbox One so that you can identify your console when there are multiple Xbox One consoles in the vicinity. After you change the name, you'll have to restart your Xbox.

- **Console Info**—Choosing this option pulls up a screen that shows you the information you need to use when registering and troubleshooting your console. It provides your serial number, console ID, OS version, and Xbox Live device ID.

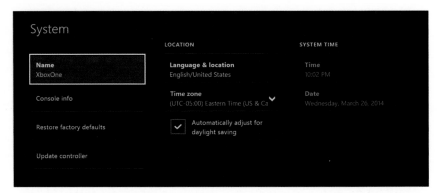

- **Restore Factory Defaults**—This option removes everything from your console so that it goes back to the system it was when you first took it out of the box. Because all accounts, apps, games, saved games (that haven't been synced to the cloud), and settings are erased, this is an option you should only use if absolutely necessary. It is not considered a troubleshooting option.

- **Update Controller**—Here, you can update your Xbox One controller with the latest software to support the use of the Xbox One Stereo Headset Adapter. This adapter connects chat or stereo headsets to your controller, such as the Xbox One Stereo Headset, third-party gaming headsets, or legacy headsets. The adapter is included with the Xbox One Stereo Headset and can also be purchased separately.

The middle section includes

- **Location**—Here, you can change the language display information of your console, such as if you move to a different time zone or region. The Language & Location option controls your console's display language and region, including for content at the Xbox Store. The Time Zone option lets you select the time zone you're in, and the Automatically Adjust for Daylight Saving option enables your console clock to change automatically with daylight saving time.

On the far right, you'll find

- **System Time**—These settings are inaccessible while you're connected to Xbox Live. During those times, your console uses "net time," which is automatically pulled from online time servers. You can change these time settings when you're not connected to Xbox Live.

Display & Sound

Your Xbox One console supports a variety of display settings, which you can adjust to best suit your TV, if needed. Because the resolution settings are selected automatically when you hook up your console, you shouldn't have to adjust these settings. Nevertheless, it's good to have an understanding of them, and they are as follows:

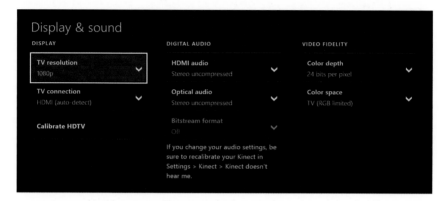

The Display options include

- **TV Resolution**—Your Xbox One console supports the following resolutions: 720p and 1080p. These are standard for high-definition TVs.

- **TV Connection**—There are three settings for handling the detection of available resolutions: HDMI (Auto-detect), which is the recommend setting because it enables your console to select the TV resolution based on information provided by your TV; DVI, which should be selected only if you're using an HDMI-to-DVI converter (keep in mind that this will disable HDMI audio, so you won't have audio unless you're using Optical Audio); and HDMI, which you can select if you know there's a resolution that's supported by both your console and TV but that resolution is not listed.

- **Calibrate HDTV**—Select this option if you want to calibrate your TV to get the best visual experience for games, movies, and TV.

The Digital Audio options include

- **HDMI Audio**—Depending on what your TV or sound system supports, select from Stereo Uncompressed, 5.1 Uncompressed, 7.1 Uncompressed, or Bitstream Out. Refer to your TV or sound system's manual to determine what's supported. You also have the option of turning off

HDMI audio. You would select this option if you're using optical audio to meet your audio needs.

- **Optical Audio**—If you have an optical audio cable going from the display or sound system to the S/PDIF port on your console, select either Stereo Uncompressed or Bitstream Out, respectively, depending on what's supported. Refer to your TV or sound system's manual if you're unsure. If nothing is plugged into your S/PDIF port, select Off to disable the port.

- **Bitstream Format**—This enables you to choose between DTS Digital Surround or Dolby Digital provided either HDMI Audio and/or Optical Audio are set to Bitstream Out.

The Video Fidelity options include

- **Color Depth**—Color depth, also known as *bit depth*, refers to the number of bits used to indicate the color of a single pixel in an image. As the number of bits increases, the number of possible colors also increases, improving picture quality. True Color displays use 24 bits of color data to represent the three RGB colors. If you know that your TV supports Deep Color, you can also choose 30 bits per pixel or 36 bits per pixel, depending on what is supported.

- **Color Space**—Microsoft highly recommends that you leave the color space setting set to TV (RGB Limited). RGB Limited is the broadcast standard for video content and is intended for use with TVs. On the other hand, if you're using a PC monitor, you can select PC (RGB Full) to optimize your display's black levels.

Closed Captioning

This area enables you to turn closed captioning on and off. If you turn it on, you can select between the default style and a custom style. There are many options for customization of captions, from selecting the type, color, and size of the captions to the background and window color.

Power & Startup

Selecting Power & Startup from the Settings menu enables you to configure your console's startup and power options, such as whether it shuts down automatically and turns on via a voice command.

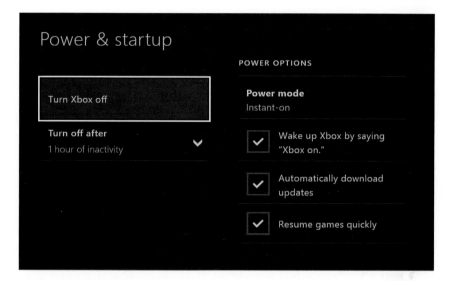

The options on the left include

- **Turn Xbox Off**—Select this option if you want to turn off your console. It just provides another way to accomplish this task.

- **Turn Off After**—This option enables you to select whether you want your console to turn off automatically after a set amount of inactivity. You can select from Turn Off After 1 Hour of Inactivity, Turn Off After 6 Hours of Inactivity, and Don't Turn Off Automatically.

The options on the right include

- **Power Mode**—You can use this to select whether you want Instant-On mode or Energy-Saving mode. Instant-On is recommended. If you select Energy-Saving mode, you won't be able to use your voice to turn on the console and your console won't automatically download updates. In addition, this mode slows the startup time and prevents you from turning on your TV and cable/satellite box with the console. When Instant-On is selected, you can still opt out of certain features, such as the ability to wake up Xbox by saying "Xbox, on" and to automatically download updates. Simply uncheck these items.

  There is also a Resume Games Quickly option. If you select it, you can resume games from the exact point you left off, even if you turn your Xbox One off and on again; however, you must sign back in to your account before you launch the game. If you don't, your console will restart the game.

Adjusting Family Settings

Under the Settings menu, there is a Family option to the right of the Console setting options. By creating a family on Xbox One, you can manage privacy and online safety settings for children. Any adult in the family can add new members to the family, and there are different rights given to adults and to children with regard to managing the family.

It's Not All Good

Microsoft Accounts and Kids

To make use of these options, each family member needs their own login account, which means they also need their own email account. This includes children. If you're not comfortable creating an email account for your child, one possibility is just to create a new Microsoft email account on the console and use it only for registration purposes.

Add Family

To add a family member, sign in to your Xbox Live account and then follow these steps:

1. Go to the Settings on your console, scroll right to the Family section, and select Add to Family.

2. Select Add New.

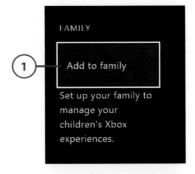

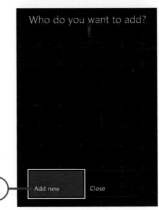

3. Have that person sign in to his or her Microsoft account (or choose to Get a New Email) using the onscreen keyboard and select Enter.

4. Have the person enter his or her password and select Enter.

5. Select Next on the privacy message that appears.

6. Have the person choose a color for his or her Dashboard tiles and select Next.

7. Confirm the person's look and
    select Next. There's really noth-
    ing you can do here other than
    accept what you see.

8. Decide whether you want to save
    the password or have the console
    keep asking for your password
    before you can log on.

9. Decide whether you want Kinect
    to sign you in. If you do, proceed
    to step 10. Otherwise, proceed to
    step 11.

10. Have the person get in front of Kinect so that it can recognize him or her. After it does, select That's Me. (If it doesn't put the name over the person's head on its own, have the person raise his or her hand straight up in the air.)

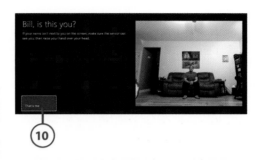

10

11. Select Add to Family.

12. The person now appears in your family on the Settings screen.

When Adding Children

If the person you're adding is a child, and you haven't already associated his or her account with yours, you'll need to provide parental consent to complete this process.

11

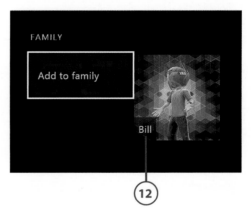

12

It's Not All Good

Can't Add Yourself to the Family?

If you're unable to add yourself to your Xbox One family, try these tips:

- Have the other adult from the Xbox One family you want to join sign in to the console and add you. You must be signed in as well.

- Make sure you haven't joined another family. You can be part of only one Xbox One family at a time. If you do belong to another family, you must have an adult from the original family remove you from that family before you can join the new family.

Remove Family

To remove a family member, follow these steps:

1. Go to Settings, scroll to Family, and select the family member you want to remove.

2. Select Remove from Family.

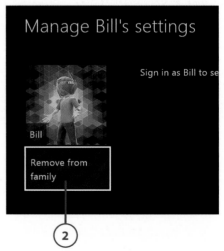

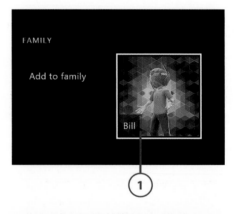

3. Confirm Remove from Family. The person's profile no longer appears under your family.

Managing Other People and Guest Settings

Under the Settings screen, you can also manage other people by removing accounts and adjusting guest settings.

Remove Accounts

To remove accounts, follow these steps:

1. Go to the Home screen, press the Menu button on your controller, select Settings, and scroll right to Other People.

2. Select Remove Accounts.

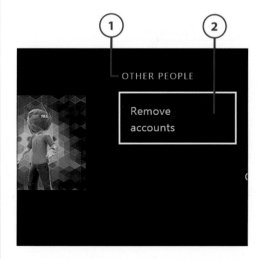

3. Scroll to the person you want to remove and select Choose This Person.

4. Select Remove from This Xbox. The person is now removed.

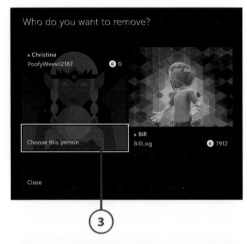

Who do you want to remove?

• Christina
PoofyWeevil2187   0

Choose this person

                        • Bill
                        BillLog   7912

Close

③

Remove PoofyWeevil2187 from this Xbox?

PoofyWeevil2187's account will be deleted from this Xbox, incl
have to enter their Microsoft account email and password.
PoofyWeevil2187's gamertag and Microsoft account will still ex
affiliation, gamerscore, and achievements.

Remove from this
Xbox   Cancel

④

Adjust Guest Settings

When guests without Xbox Live accounts want to play games or watch movies on your Xbox One, you can sign them in with a guest account and they can use your console without you being present or signed in. To facilitate this, create a guest key, which enables the guest to override any content limitations that you set as the default experience on your Xbox One.

To set a guest key, sign in to your profile and then follow these steps:

1. Press the Menu button on your controller, select Settings, and then scroll to the far right to Guest Settings.

2. Select Create a Guest Key.

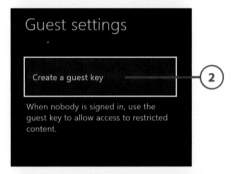

Guest Keys Versus Passkeys

Setting a guest key doesn't grant access to accounts for which you've already set a personal passkey. To optimize security, Microsoft recommends that you use a different six-digit combination for the guest key.

3. Set your six-digit guest key using the buttons on your console as illustrated onscreen.

4. Enter the guest key again to confirm it.

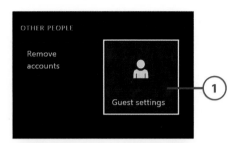

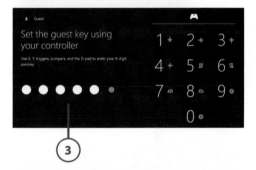

5. At the Guest Settings screen, decide what kind of access to content your guests should have and whether people can download and make new accounts. Then press the B button to get back to the Settings menu or the Xbox button to go to the Home screen.

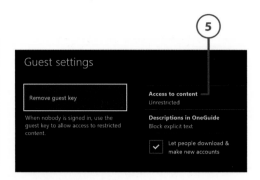

UNDERSTANDING RESTRICTIONS

>>>Go Further

If you are signed in to your console along with your guest, your privacy and safety settings will apply to your gaming session. If multiple family members are signed in, the console will enforce any rules that the adults in the household have set, which means that the most restrictive settings are likely to apply. In addition, any content restrictions you set for guests also apply to searches and content on the Xbox Store.

Multitasking with Snap

Snap is an Xbox One feature that enables you to multitask by letting you anchor, or snap, the apps most important to you to the right side of the screen while you're engaged in another activity. For example, say you're in the mood to play a football game but also want to keep tabs on the live game going on. No problem! With Snap, you can continue playing your game and have live TV snapped and streaming on the right side of your screen. If suddenly that live game gets super exciting, you can switch over to that snapped app and view it in Full-Screen mode. Pretty cool!

And just as there are multiple ways to skin a cat (though we're not sure why anyone would want to do that), there are multiple ways for you to snap/ unsnap apps and switch which app you're focusing on. Just remember that although games can have a snapped app, games themselves can't be snapped. Also, it's one size fits all, as there's no way to resize either the main window or the snapped app.

Snap and Unsnap Apps

Follow these steps to snap an app
with your controller:

1. Go to the Home screen and select
   the Snap tile.

2. You now see a list of apps you can
   snap. Select the app you want.
   That's it. To unsnap, proceed to
   step 3.

3. Go back to the Home screen and
   select the Snap tile again; it'll say
   Unsnap.

>>>Go Further

SNAPPING/UNSNAPPING WITH VOICE OR GESTURES

To use your voice to snap an app, follow these steps:

1. Say "Xbox, Snap."

2. Now say the name of a listed app that you want to snap. To unsnap that app using your voice, proceed to step 3.

3. Say "Xbox, unsnap."

Follow these steps to use motion controls to snap an app:

1. At the Xbox Home screen, clasp your hands as though you're gripping the edges of your screen.

2. Pull those edges toward your chest.

3. Now hover and press your hand forward on the Snap tile.

4. Then hover and press your hand forward on the app you want to snap. To unsnap using gestures, repeat steps 1–4.

Switch Over to Your Snapped App

The easiest ways to switch focus of which app you're in is to either double-tap the Xbox button on your controller or to say "Xbox, switch." Now the previously snapped app is the larger app in the center of your screen, with the other app appearing off to the right side.

An alternative way to toggle between your primary and snapped apps using your controller is to press the Xbox button to go Home, move to the app you want to focus on, and press the A button.

View a Snapped App in Full Screen

Your Xbox One remembers the most recent size of any app you've used. So if you want to view an app that you've snapped, it will appear in those snapped dimensions. To have that app fill your entire screen, follow these steps on your controller:

1. From the Home screen, go to the app that you want to view in full screen.

2. Press the Menu button on your controller and select Go Full Screen.

Find out about all the features that Xbox Live makes possible

Learn about the different Xbox Live membership levels

In this chapter, you learn about Xbox Live and the different membership levels, earning achievements, accessing your account on other consoles, and how updates work.

3

Examining Xbox Live

Xbox Live is a Microsoft service that enables online multiplayer gaming, access to various digital media and services, and system and app updates. It was first made available in 2002 for the original Xbox console and has evolved considerably since then, with new features added regularly, including expansion of the service to other platforms, such as computers and mobile devices. It is available both as a limited free service and as a subscription-based service with a wide range of benefits. Joining Xbox Live and maintaining an Xbox Live Gold membership is crucial to getting the most out of your console.

Understanding Xbox Live Memberships

The free Xbox Live service is known as *Xbox Live Free* (it was previously known as *Xbox Live Silver*), whereas the paid service is known as *Xbox Live Gold*, with the latter offering access to considerably more features and services, as demonstrated in Table 3.1. As a bonus, the same Xbox Live account works across other Microsoft platforms, including the Xbox 360.

Games with Gold

Games with Gold provides Xbox Live Gold members with at least two free games each month. Originally a limited-time promotion for the Xbox 360, Microsoft has confirmed that the service will continue and offer similar benefits for the Xbox One starting in late 2014.

Although an Xbox Live Gold membership makes many more features and services accessible to you on your Xbox One, several have additional requirements (for example, a Netflix subscription to access Netflix content). In addition, much of the digital content on the various digital marketplaces on offer is not free. For example, the only downloadable games that are generally free are ad-supported games or online multiplayer titles that offer in-game purchases. Making purchases from any of the marketplaces requires having an existing balance, using a prepaid card or code, or having a credit card or PayPal account on file. See the "Redeeming Codes" and "Paying for Purchases with PayPal" sections later in this chapter for more information.

Table 3.1   Sample Comparison of Features and Services Offered by Xbox Live Free Versus Xbox Live Gold

Feature	Xbox Live Free	Xbox Live Gold	Additional Requirements
Avatar creation and customization	Yes	Yes	None
Bing	Yes	Yes	None
Downloadable games and game add-ons	Yes	Yes	None
Family settings	Yes	Yes	None

Feature	Xbox Live Free	Xbox Live Gold	Additional Requirements
Free demos and game previews	Yes	Yes	None
Voice chat	Yes	Yes	Headset or Kinect
Xbox Video	Yes	Yes	None
Amazon Instant Video	No	Yes	Amazon Prime subscription
ESPN	No	Yes	WatchESPN-affiliated ISP
Game DVR	No	Yes	None
Hulu Plus	No	Yes	Hulu Plus account
Internet Explorer	No	Yes	None
Netflix	No	Yes	Netflix account
NFL on Xbox	No	Yes	Cable or satellite provider subscription
OneGuide	No	Yes	None
Online multiplayer gaming	No	Yes	None
Party chat	No	Yes	Headset or Kinect
Skype	No	Yes	Kinect and a Skype account
SmartMatch	No	Yes	None
Twitch.tv	No	Yes	Twitch.tv account
Upload Studio	No	Yes	None
Xbox Music	No	Yes	Xbox Music Pass subscription

You can purchase an Xbox Live Gold membership directly through your Xbox One, but you will likely save some money if you shop around. Check other retailers before you buy, such as game stores and online merchants. At Amazon.com, for instance, you can opt to purchase a card that contains a code that gives you access to Xbox Live for a certain amount of time, or you can opt to receive the code via email once you make your payment. If using a third-party retailer, just be sure to use one that is reputable, especially if you opt to receive your code electronically.

Joining Xbox Live

If you would like to go beyond the default free account, you can sign up for an Xbox Live Gold membership directly on the console. Follow these steps to get your Xbox Live Gold membership:

1. Go to the Home screen.

2. Press the Menu button on the controller and select Settings.

   Alternatively, you can say "Xbox, go to settings," from any screen, or select the Settings tile on the Home screen.

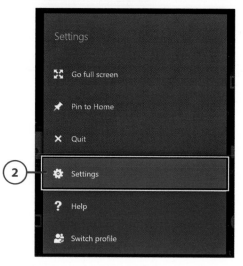

3. Select Subscriptions.

4. Press the A button on the controller to select Learn About Gold Membership.

5. Press the A button to continue past the unnecessary promo screen.

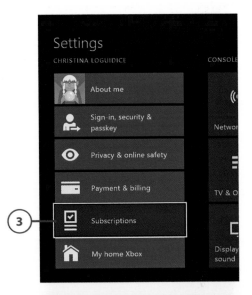

6. If you want to select one of the available membership options, select a displayed option and then proceed to step 7. If you have a code, select Use a Code and see the next section, "Redeeming Codes." If you want to decline signing up, select No Thanks to return to step 4. (From there, you can press the B button to back out of the Subscriptions settings.)

7. If you don't already have a credit card on file, select Add a Credit Card to enter your credit card information.

Each year, your membership automatically renews at the current rate. To cancel auto renewal, log in at xbox.com/accounts. See the "Connecting to Xbox on the Web" section later in this chapter for more information about accessing Xbox information on the Web.

8. Enter the requested information in each remaining onscreen step, starting with the cardholder's name. Your Xbox Live Gold membership is now active for the specified period.

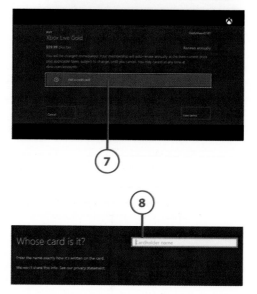

Redeeming Codes

Prepaid codes are an alternative to making digital Xbox One purchases with a credit card or PayPal account, and also a way to redeem giveaways and other promotions. These codes are available from a variety of retailers and can be redeemed for digital content in Xbox One's Games, Movies & TV, Music, and Apps stores; these codes can also be used to start or extend an Xbox Live Gold membership. On the Xbox 360, prepaid codes were limited to manually entering a 25-character code. Now, on the Xbox One, you can choose to manually enter the 25-character code, or you can instead choose to use Kinect to quickly scan a QR code containing the same information.

What Is a QR Code?

QR codes stand for Quick Response codes. These codes are special, two-dimensional bar codes that have become popular with some smartphone users for quickly displaying text-based information or going to a specific web address. Thanks to the Xbox One's Use a Code functionality and the Kinect's built-in camera, you can have that same convenient smartphone, camera, and app experience on your console.

Scanning Codes

If your console is on and Kinect is enabled, simply say, "Xbox, use a code." Kinect will view your room and wait for you to hold up a QR code from a redemption card, printout, or mobile device to its camera. As long as you're holding the QR code within 6 feet of the camera, Kinect should recognize and automatically redeem the code within a few seconds.

It's Not All Good

Sometimes when trying to scan a QR code displayed on your smartphone or other mobile screen, it just doesn't work. If you run into problems, you might need to turn down the screen's brightness to help Kinect better see the code.

As an alternative to the Kinect voice command, you can select the Use a Code tile in the Games store.

Select this option in the Games store
to scan or manually enter a code

Enter a Code Manually

Besides redeeming a code from the Use a Code tile in the Xbox One Games store, you can also use a web browser. This is particularly handy for older redemption cards that lack a QR code or when you're away from your Xbox One.

From your computer, smartphone, or tablet web browser, go to https://account.xbox.com/en-US/ PaymentAndBilling/RedeemCode and follow these steps:

1. Click the Redeem button.

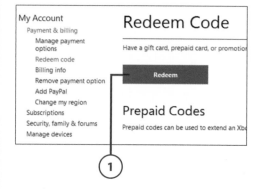

2. Enter your Xbox Live credentials, then click the Sign In button.

3. Enter your 25-character code, then click the Confirm button.

4. Click the Confirm button.

Although somewhat superfluous, these steps also work from the Xbox One's Internet Explorer app.

Please enter your email address in the format someone@example.com.

Microsoft account What's this?

someone@example.com

········

☐ Keep me signed in

Sign in

②

Enter your code

25-character code

Confirm   Cancel

③

USE PREPAID CODE

Prepaid 12M Xbox LIVE Gold

Prepaid code

Subject to the Xbox Live terms of use and xbox.com/usagerules.

Confirm   Cancel

④

SMARTGLASS

Another alternative to manually entering the code on your console with your controller is using the SmartGlass app to enter the code from your smartphone or tablet. Although not quite as handy an alternative as using a web browser, it's nice to have yet another option for redeeming codes. Refer to Chapter 11, "Looking Through the SmartGlass," for more on SmartGlass.

Paying for Purchases with PayPal

PayPal, a wholly owned subsidiary of eBay, is one of the most popular online payment services on the Internet. The service enables users to send and receive money from associated bank accounts or credit cards.

Although you can easily add a credit card and billing address from the Payment & Billing section of Settings right on your console (see "Breaking Down the Settings Screen" in Chapter 2, "Navigating Your Xbox One's Dashboard and Settings"), if you want to leverage the convenience of a PayPal account, you need to do it from a web browser.

Connecting PayPal and Your Xbox One

From your computer, smartphone, tablet, or Xbox One Internet Explorer web browser, go to https://account.xbox.com/en-US/PaymentAndBilling/AddPayPal and follow these steps:

1. Enter your Xbox Live credentials, and then click the Sign In button.

⊗ XBOX

Please enter your email address in the format someone@example.com.

Microsoft account What's this?

someone@example.com

••••••••

☐ Keep me signed in

Sign in

①

2. Click Next.

3. If you already have a PayPal account, select Pay with My PayPal Account and enter the requested information. You're now finished. If you need to obtain a PayPal account, proceed to step 4.

4. Enter the required information under Create a PayPal Account.

5. When finished entering the information, click on Agree and Create Account.

When you're finished, and after logging in to your Xbox One, your PayPal account will be listed under Payment Options in the Payment & Billing section under Settings, along with any credit cards. When it comes time to pay for a digital transaction, you can then quickly use your PayPal account or any of the other associated payment options.

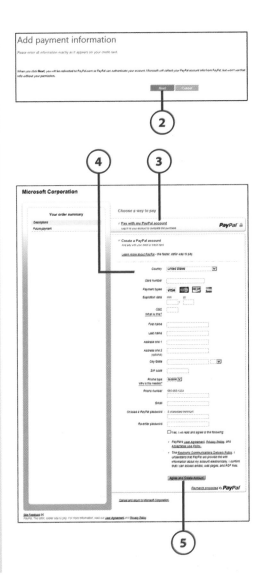

Earning Achievements for Games and Media

Achievements are awarded for completing specific activities in a game. The required actions vary by title and could be anything from completing a game without using a certain weapon, to winning a certain number of online matches, to completing a game, or even by dying a certain way. In short, achievements are up to the individual game developer's imagination and are a great incentive for getting the most out of a particular game or app.

Completing achievements boosts your gamerscore, which is an achievement system for bragging rights, and sometimes provides other rewards, like specific in-game perks. There are also challenges, which are timed events for games and apps that are usually geared toward completing new tasks. Although challenges don't boost your gamerscore, they can bring other types of recognition and in-game benefits.

Some challenges are tied to media achievements instead of just games, as it was on the Xbox 360. These often take the form of watching specific TV shows and movies or rating content in apps like Netflix, Hulu Plus, Crackle, Amazon Instant Video, and Redbox Instant. Like challenges, these media achievements don't affect your gamerscore, but they do show up in your list of achievements and are a fun way to game-ify your media consumption.

You can see what achievements and challenges are available and what you've already earned by doing one of the following:

- Select the Achievements tile on the Home screen (if present).
- If Kinect is active, say "Xbox, go to achievements."
- Select the Social tile and then Achievements.

Present gamerscore

Profile   Select the Achievements tile to see what achievements and challenges are available

The Achievements screen is broken up into three sections. The first section is Featured Challenges, where all of the timed challenges reside.

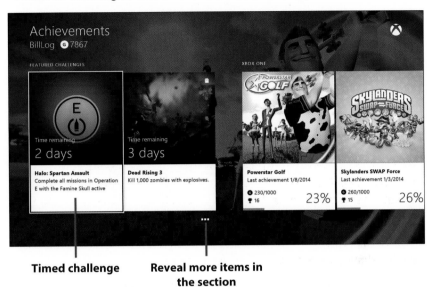

Timed challenge   **Reveal more items in the section**

The second section is Xbox One, where all Xbox One game, app, and media achievements are listed.

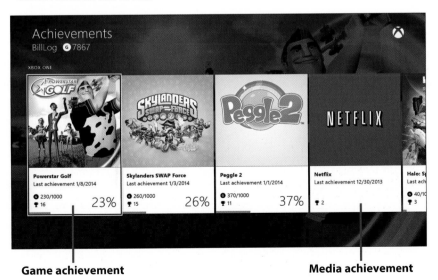

Game achievement   **Media achievement**

The third section is Other Achievements, where your achievements from other Xbox Live-compatible platforms, like the Xbox 360, are listed.

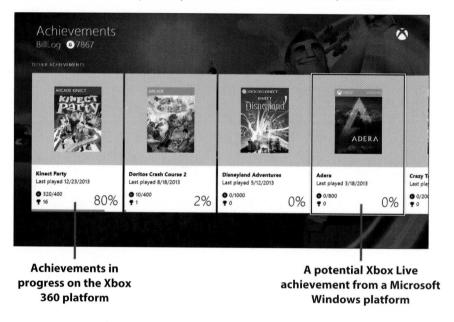

Achievements in progress on the Xbox 360 platform

A potential Xbox Live achievement from a Microsoft Windows platform

Selecting any of the tiles reveals how far away you are from any goals, what challenges remain, what achievements have already been unlocked, and what achievements remain locked.

Accessing Xbox Live Gold Anywhere

With an Xbox Live Gold account, any other local users of your home console, be they family or friends, will have access to your account's purchased games, as well as multiplayer gaming and app options, even if they don't have an Xbox Live Gold account of their own. In turn, if you log in to an Internet-connected Xbox One with your Xbox Live Gold account at a family member or friend's house, you can still enjoy full access to your profile, digital games, and apps, even if they don't have an Xbox Live Gold account. As a further bonus, you can be logged in to your Xbox Live Gold account on both an Xbox One and Xbox 360 simultaneously, but not two Xbox Ones.

Connecting to Xbox on the Web

Besides accessing various account and billing information on your console and through the Xbox One SmartGlass mobile apps (see Chapter 11), you can also visit the www.xbox.com website from your favorite browser. After logging in, you'll see My Account and Profile, Activity Feed, Friends, Messages, and code redemption (Redeem Code) options that apply to your Xbox Live account and any applicable Xbox One and Xbox 360 consoles:

Select one of these options for marketing and promotional information related to the chosen topic　　　**Search Xbox.com**　　　**Click on your profile name to see your profile summary**

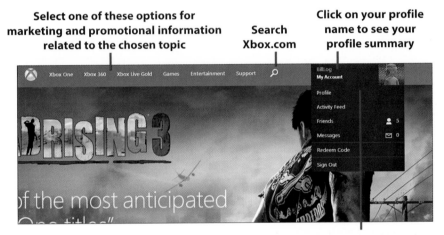

Hover the cursor to see the additional options below My Account on a desktop browser, or tap the three lines on a mobile browser

- **My Account**—Selecting this option provides a summary of your recent digital transactions and active subscriptions, as well as links to adjust payment and billing information, and device-specific options such as console registration and repair status.

- **Profile**—Selecting this option provides Xbox One SmartGlass download links for Windows, Windows Phone, Apple iOS, and Android platforms. If you would like access to your actual profile information, including recent activity and editing options for your profile and avatar, click on your green profile name above My Account.

- **Activity Feed**—Selecting this option displays recent activity, including games played and apps accessed.

- **Friends**—Selecting this option displays pending friend requests and friends who are either presently online and offline, as well as their most recent activity. You can use the Find option to search all gamertags and then either send a message or friend request if they're not already a friend.

- **Messages**—Select this option to send a message to one or more friends from your existing list of friends.

- **Redeem Code**—Selecting this option displays the screen where you redeem a gift card, prepaid card, or promotional code. See the "Enter a Code Manually" section earlier in this chapter for more information on redeeming codes from this screen.

- **Sign Out**—Selecting this option immediately logs you out. Select Sign In to log in again.

Issues with Xbox Live, Services, or Apps?

If you notice issues with Xbox Live or services and apps for either the Xbox One or Xbox 360, use your browser to log in to http://support.xbox.com/en-US/xbox-live-status. Every possible service and app is listed with its current status of either "up and running" or one of several possible error or maintenance states.

Enjoying Xbox Live Rewards

As part of your Xbox Live Gold membership, you can sign up for Xbox Live Rewards. Xbox Live Rewards provides extra incentives, such as Rewards Credits or prizes, for taking surveys, playing games, watching videos, and doing various other activities on your Xbox One. Earn enough Rewards Credits and you'll be able to convert those credits to money to purchase digital goods from the various Xbox One stores. To join Xbox Live Rewards, use your web browser to go to www.xbox.com/en-US/live/rewards?xr=shellnav and click on the Join Xbox Live Rewards button.

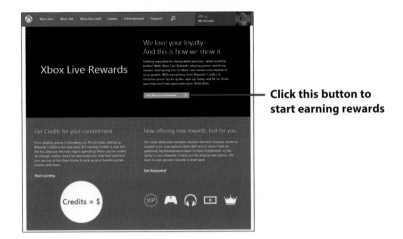

**Click this button to
start earning rewards**

Understanding Updates

With today's fast-moving technology, updates are inevitable, and that
includes updates for both your console and its games and apps. These
updates either fix bugs or add new features (sometimes both), and, unfortunately, eventually become mandatory. If you choose not to accept a mandatory update, you will no longer be allowed to connect online. For a particular
game or app, this might not be a deal breaker, but if it's a console update,
this means all online functionality will be disabled. In short, unless you have a
very good reason for avoiding an available update, as a certain sports apparel
company likes to say, just do it.

Change your gamerpic

Customize your profile

CTORSLOG5
Appearing offline

G 0

Friends	Followers		Reputation
12	1		Good

Appearing offline ▼

Choose color

Customize avatar

Set gamerpic

Set gamertag

Privacy settings

In this chapter, you learn about personalizing your Xbox One experience, including how you're virtually represented and about some must-have accessories for your console.

→ Understanding Your Profile

→ Building an Avatar

→ Assigning a Profile to a Wireless Controller

→ Accessorizing Your Xbox One

Personalizing Your Xbox One Experience

Your Xbox One is thoughtfully equipped to give you a personalized experience. Not only can you create your own user profile, complete with a gamerpic (gamer picture), but you can also create an avatar to represent you, set a gamertag (your gamer name), customize your Home screen, and create your own circle of friends.

In addition, there are many accessories you can consider buying to deck out your console and Kinect to enrich your overall experience. In this chapter, you learn how to personalize and accessorize your Xbox One so that you have all the right enhancements and add-ons.

Understanding Your Profile

Your profile, which establishes your presence on your Xbox One, includes several components, including your gamerpic, gamertag, and avatar. How you set up your profile also determines the color of the tiles on your Home screen when you are logged in, your privacy settings, and whether you appear online or offline on Xbox Live. Any profile you want to have Xbox Live Gold access needs an Xbox Live Gold account. For more on Xbox Live, turn to Chapter 3, "Examining Xbox Live." Profiles without Xbox Live Gold have no dependence on or interactivity with the Xbox Live Gold service, although they still require an associated Microsoft Account.

If you already have an Xbox Live Gold account because you previously had an Xbox 360, your profile, account information, family settings, and music and video content are automatically transferred to your Xbox One when you sign in to your account. If you do not have an Xbox Live Gold account, but you followed the steps in "Power On for the First Time" from Chapter 1, "Setting Up Your Xbox One," your Xbox One already gave you a basic profile, including a gamertag and gamerpic that you can modify.

Get into Your Profile

It is easy to customize your existing profile on your Xbox One console. To access your profile, follow these steps:

1. From the Home screen, select Sign In.

2. Select the profile you want to customize.

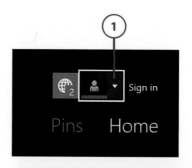

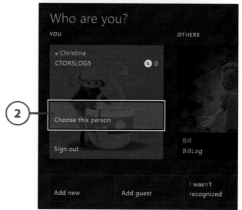

3. When Xbox returns you to the Home screen, select your Social tile.

4. Select My Profile.

5. You are now in your profile and can make the desired modifications, which are reviewed in the next section, "Customizing Your Profile."

Customizing Your Profile

When you're at the Profile screen, the following customization options are available to you:

- **Appear Offline/Appear Online**—When you select this option, you toggle between "Appear offline" and "Appear online." If you don't want anyone to know that you're online, select Appear Offline.

- **Choose Color**—This option enables you to select the color of the tiles on the Home screen. At the time of this writing, there are 21 options to choose from. Simply scroll to the color you like until it is outlined in black and press the A button to select it. If multiple people are using your console, you might want each person to select his or her own color.

- **Customize Avatar**—Your avatar is a digital representation of you, and you can change how your avatar looks at any time. For more on creating an avatar, turn to the "Building an Avatar" section later in this chapter.

- **Set Gamerpic**—Xbox One introduces new, full-screen, 1080p gamerpics. Your gamerpic is the image that represents you. When you select this option, you can choose from any of the available gamerpics, and you can change your gamerpic as many times as you want. There are countless images to choose from, from food, to creatures of every kind, to symbols, to abstract art, to numbers. Simply scroll to the image you like until it is outlined in black and press the A button to select it. If you don't like any of the options, you can make one with your avatar. For more on that, see the "Create a Gamerpic with Your Avatar" section later in this chapter.

- **Set Gamertag**—Here, you can change your gamertag, which is the name associated with your Xbox Live account. You have only one chance to change your gamertag for free; thereafter, you need to pay if you want to set a new one. For instructions on how to set a gamertag, see the "Change a Gamertag" section next.

- **Privacy Settings**—Selecting this option brings you to your Privacy & Online Safety settings. For more on the options here, turn to "Breaking Down the Settings Screen" in Chapter 2, "Navigating Your Xbox One's Dashboard and Settings."

Change a Gamertag

Changing your gamertag is easy as pie! Just keep in mind, as previously mentioned, you can do it only once for free, so you must be careful when making your selection. To change your gamertag, follow these steps:

1. Go to the Profile screen and select Set Gamertag. If needed, follow steps 1 to 5 in the "Get into Your Profile" section earlier in this chapter.

2. Xbox provides six alternative gamertags. To see more auto-generated options, select More; every time you select this option, six new potential gamertags appear onscreen. Select the option you want, and proceed to step 5.

3. If you don't like any of the suggested gamertags, create a personalized gamertag by selecting Make My Own, and proceed to step 4.

4. Use the onscreen keyboard to input your proposed gamertag, and then select Enter.

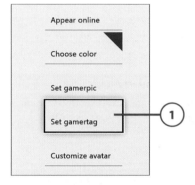

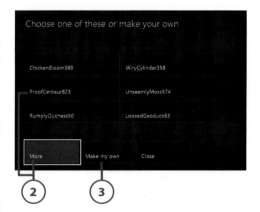

5. At the Change Gamertag screen, select Sounds Good if you're happy with your gamertag. If not, select Go Back and enter a new gamertag, and then select Sounds Good.

6. You now have your new gamertag. Select Close to go back to the Profile screen.

>>>Go Further

WHAT'S IN A NAME?

With more than 50 million Xbox Live members and counting, it is becoming increasingly difficult to create a gamertag name that's not already spoken for. It might be tempting to create a gamertag with random letters or other gibberish to ensure no one else has selected it, but keep in mind that that can make your name difficult for your friends to find. A better strategy is to try to add a few numbers to your preferred gamertag, or simply choose one of the suggested names.

Building an Avatar

Although avatars are supported on Xbox One, their role has been minimized. Unlike on the Xbox 360, where they are heavily integrated into the interface, they largely remain hidden on the Xbox One outside of the Friends app (see Chapter 6, "Making the Social Connection") and are mainly used in gamer-pics, which is reviewed in "Create a Gamerpic with Your Avatar" later in this chapter.

Still, building your digital representation can be lots of fun and is a bit like a game itself. After all, you can shape and mold your avatar to take on what-ever identity you want, and if you change your mind about your avatar's features, you can make modifications simply by pressing a few buttons, enabling you to test a variety of looks.

Select a Base to Work From

Before you can start customizing your avatar, you must select a base model to work with. Go to your Pro-file screen, as described earlier in the "Get into Your Profile" section, and follow these steps to get started:

1. On the Profile screen, select Customize Avatar.

2. You now see all the bases from which you can work. Select the left and right arrows to scroll through additional options until you find the one you want.

3. Select the avatar you want to use as your base model. (You can change everything about the avatar you pick.)

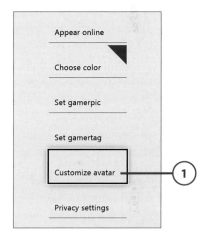

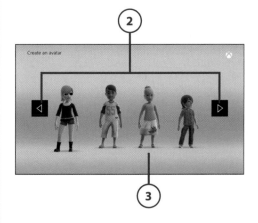

Change My Features

Once you have your base avatar selected, as described in the "Select a Base to
Work From" section, you can change its
appearance by modifying its facial features, body size, and coloring. To make
modifications to your avatar, follow
these steps:

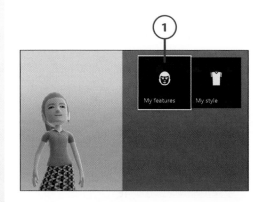

1. Select the My Features tile.

2. Use the left stick or D-pad to
    move between assorted catego-
    ries, such as Body, Hair, Eyebrows,
    Eyes, Ears, Nose, Mouth, Chin,
    Facial Features, and Colors (where
    you can change colors of skin,
    eyes, hair, and so on).

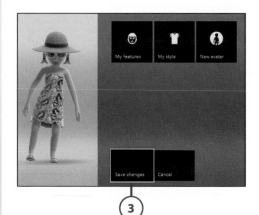

Navigation Guide

Each of these categories uses the
same controls for navigation. Use the
left stick or D-pad to move between
the various options. When you find
a feature that you want (such as a
particular mouth shape in the Mouth
category), highlight it and press the
A button to select it. You can use the
left and right triggers to rotate your
avatar for a better look. If you change
your mind at any time, press the B
button on your controller or select
Cancel at the bottom of the screen.

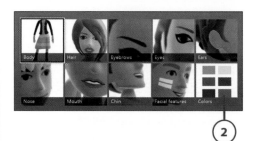

3. Press the B button to return to the
    Avatar Customization screen, and
    then select Save Changes. Your
    avatar is now saved.

It's Not All Good

Don't Lose Your Avatar

When you save your avatar, a new option appears on the Avatar Customization screen: New Avatar. Although it might seem you can build an unlimited number of avatars if you select this option, your avatar in fact disappears and is replaced by any new avatar you save. If you don't want to lose your avatar after selecting this option, press the B button on your controller to exit the screen.

Change My Style

To change the style of your avatar, if you're not already at the Avatar Customization screen, follow steps 1 to 5 in the "Get into Your Profile" section, and then select Customize Avatar. If you want to change your avatar's clothing, makeup, and accessories, follow these steps:

1. At the Avatar Customization screen, select My Style.

2. Use your left stick or D-pad to move between the 10 categories. Select a category by pressing the A button on your controller. The options include Dress Up, Hats & More, Tops, Bottoms, Shoes, Glasses, Earrings, Wristwear, Rings, and Gloves.

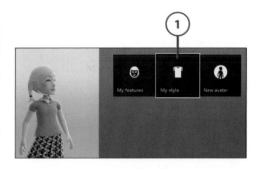

Navigation Guide

Navigating between each of the My Style categories requires the same controls. Use the left stick or D-pad to move between the various items. Use the left and right triggers to rotate your avatar for a better look. If you change your mind at any time, press the B button on your controller or select Cancel onscreen to go back. Press the A button to make your selection and return to the My Style screen.

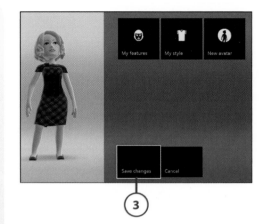

3. When you are finished setting your style, press the B button to return to the Avatar Customization screen and select Save Changes.

Not Enough Gear?

You can purchase items for your avatar online. Visit the Avatar Editor at https://live.xbox.com/en-US/AvatarEditor.

Create a Gamerpic with Your Avatar

After you've created and saved your avatar, you can show it off in a gamerpic. Follow these steps:

1. If you've just finished and saved your avatar, select Make a Gamerpic. Otherwise, go to your profile (follow steps 1 to 5 from the "Get into Your Profile" section) and select Customize Avatar, and then Make a Gamerpic, or go to Set Gamerpic and select the Make One with Your Avatar tile in the lower-left corner.

2. Select the pose you want; the selected pose is highlighted with a checkmark. Then use the right stick on your controller to position your avatar left, right, up, and down, depending on what you want to have in frame. When satisfied, press the B button on your controller.

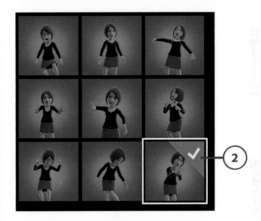

3. Customize the pose by turning your avatar left or right, zooming out and in, and changing the background. If changing the background, select Change Background and see step 4. Otherwise, proceed to step 5.

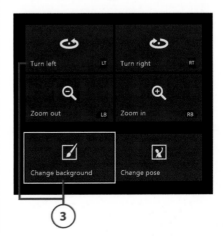

4. Select your desired background.

5. Select Save Gamerpic.

6. At the Set This as Your Gamerpic? screen, select Yes.

7. Select OK, and then press B on your controller to go back.

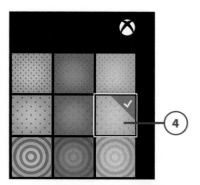

It's Not All Good

Gamerpics: Only One at a Time

If you select Email Picture from the Pose Customization screen, you automatically email the photo to the email address assigned to your Microsoft account. This is the only way to truly save additional gamerpics of your avatar because if you don't set an image as your gamerpic, there is nowhere to retrieve it. However, this might change in the future as the system is refined and the Microsoft website improves to better distinguish between the Xbox 360 and Xbox One.

Assigning a Profile to a Wireless Controller

You can automatically pair or manually assign your profile to your specific Xbox One wireless controller. Doing so puts your profile in control of the action on your console, which is especially important if multiple people are using your console at the same time. This also helps ensure that everyone has the best experience and correctly assigned achievements.

Automatically Assigning a Profile

Follow these steps to automatically assign a profile to a wireless controller:

1. Press the Xbox button on the controller you want to use.

2. Stand approximately 6 feet away from your Kinect sensor and point your controller toward it so that Kinect can detect your controller's infrared signal.

3. Kinect should now recognize you and automatically assign you to the controller you're holding.

It's Not All Good

Having Issues Getting the Profile Assigned?

If you're having issues getting the profile assigned, check the following: (1) that your Kinect is plugged in and turned on, (2) that the profile you want assigned to the controller has been set up to be recognized by Kinect (see "Use Kinect" in Chapter 1), and (3) that your controller is synced to the console (see Chapter 1). If all else fails, try to manually make the connection (see the following section, "Manually Assigning a Profile").

Manually Assigning a Profile

If you don't want to automatically pair your profile with your controller by using Kinect or you have a guest over who wants to use a controller (up to eight controllers can be connected at one time), you can manually sign in using any wireless controller.

To do so, power on the controller you want to use, go to the Dashboard, and sign in to the profile you want to use. The controller you're using is now assigned to that profile for this particular session. If you sign out again and someone else signs in using that controller, it becomes associated with that profile instead.

Accessorizing Your Xbox One

Even though your Xbox One comes with everything you need to make it work straight out of the box, there are a variety of accessories available that can make your experience even better.

Let's take a look at some of the more useful and fun accessories for your Xbox One.

Controllers

For the best and most versatile in-game control, it's hard to beat the superb wireless controller that comes with your system. Adding one or more additional Xbox One wireless controllers to your console is the ideal way for other family members and friends to join you on the couch for some great multi-player gaming. Of course, as with special cosmetic variations of the console itself, special editions of the standard wireless controller can also make a great addition to your controller lineup, so they're worth keeping an eye out for.

This striking limited-edition controller, themed to the hit game Titanfall, was the first special-edition Xbox One controller

It's hard to argue with the excellent battery life that two good AA batteries provide in the standard controller, but there are rechargeable, reusable alternatives that give similar performance. Microsoft makes the most popular option, the Xbox One Play & Charge Kit, which consists of a rechargeable battery pack that sits flush with the back of the controller and a USB cable for charging. The Xbox One Play & Charge Kit also comes as a bundle with the standard controller and offers a small savings over buying each item separately.

The Xbox One Play & Charge Kit comes with a battery that sits flush in the controller and a USB cable for charging and wired play

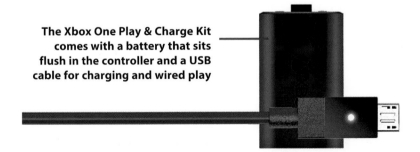

Other rechargeable options include the Energizer 2X Charging System, Energizer Power & Play Charging System, and the Nyko Charge Base, each of which comes with battery packs for two controllers as well as a stand to dock the controllers for charging.

Perhaps even more exciting, there are also some specialty controllers that are worth checking out, such as arcade sticks and steering wheels. Naturally, neither option is ideal for every game, but for specific genres. For example, the arcade stick is excellent for fighting games and the steering wheel is great for racing games. When playing games in these genres, the specialty controllers make a huge difference.

A good arcade stick option is the Mad Catz Arcade FightStick Tournament Edition 2 for Xbox One. Besides the Killer Instinct-themed artwork, you'll also take notice of the high-quality components and arcade authentic control layout.

Mad Catz's Arcade FightStick Tournament Edition 2 for Xbox One features arcade-quality Sanwa Denshi parts that are all user serviceable

A superior steering wheel control option is the Thrustmaster: TX Racing Wheel, Ferrari 458 Italia Edition. Although the name is a mouthful, you won't have too much time to think about it as you feel the powerful force feedback effects when tearing around the track in your favorite racing game.

The Thrustmaster: TX Racing Wheel features metal gas and brake pedals and gear-sequential paddle shifters

Although every Xbox One game is optimized for use with the standard wireless controller or Kinect, many computer gamers still swear by the extra precision that a mouse and keyboard provide. For this group, IOGEAR offers the KeyMander, which enables you to configure a standard USB mouse and keyboard to control your favorite games.

Keyboards

It's only Chapter 4 and you've probably already become frustrated by how tedious it can be to enter text using the controller. Although SmartGlass, which is covered in Chapter 11, "Looking Through the SmartGlass," is a rather sophisticated alternative, a good old-fashioned USB keyboard still makes for a nice option.

The USB ports on your console are ideal for plugging in standard USB keyboards, like the one you probably use with your computer. The best part is that you don't have to do anything extra to make them work after you plug them in. You can even go wireless, using your keyboard's wireless USB adapter (if it has one) as long as the Xbox One recognizes the particular keyboard make and model. (Most models from Microsoft and Logitech do work with the Xbox One.)

Universal Remotes

Even though Kinect paired with the standard wireless controller that comes with your system does a fine job when it comes to navigating menus and, of course, playing games, it's not quite as intuitive for controlling music and videos. That's where a universal remote might come in handy. Using your system's IR receiver, a compatible remote control will let you easily do things like play, pause, and rewind your media, as well as duplicate many of the functions found on the standard controller, like the Xbox button.

At launch, there was no official solution from Microsoft, but the popular Logitech Harmony line of remotes immediately provided compatible codes. In the spring of 2014, Microsoft finally released its own media remote, which provides quick access to OneGuide, DVD and Blu-ray video, streaming video, apps, TV power, and volume controls.

Microsoft's Xbox Media Remote is inexpensive and has features specifically designed around the Xbox One's capabilities

Of course, thanks to Kinect, your Xbox One also acts like an IR blaster, capable of sending its own control commands throughout your room to your television or sound system. This functionality can be further enhanced by connecting a physical IR blaster to the IR Out on the back of your console, which can be used to reach components that otherwise might be blocked from view. IR blasters typically vary only by cable length and number of emitters, and are a great way to reach components that Kinect would otherwise have trouble targeting.

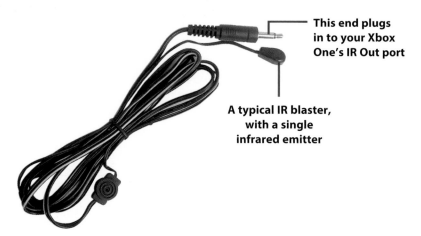

This end plugs in to your Xbox One's IR Out port

A typical IR blaster, with a single infrared emitter

Headphones and Speakers

Your Xbox One supports a nice range of sound output options, including uncompressed stereo and 5.1 (five speakers plus one subwoofer) and 7.1 (seven speakers plus one subwoofer) surround formats. If your TV speakers lack punch, a wide range of headphones and speaker systems—including everything from single soundbars to multispeaker extravaganzas—will help you take better advantage of your Xbox One's impressive audio capabilities. As a nice bonus, if you hook your cable or satellite receiver box into your Xbox One, you can hear its output through not only the Xbox One's HDMI Out, but also its S/PDIF optical audio port at the same time. This means that if you have headphones or a headphone receiver plugged in to the Xbox One's S/PDIF port, you'll not only hear the Xbox One's output but also that of your cable or satellite box, all without disturbing the audio that's output over HDMI.

Perhaps the most convenient headset option is Microsoft's Xbox One Stereo Headset, which comes with the Stereo Headset Adapter. The Stereo Headset Adapter plugs in to the bottom of the standard wireless controller and has touch button controls that let you balance game and chat audio levels, control the master volume, and mute the microphone. The Stereo Headset Adapter is also available for purchase separately and lets you use your own compatible stereo headset, though one with a microphone is required for chat.

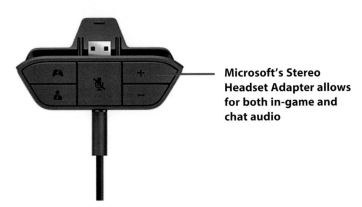

Microsoft's Stereo Headset Adapter allows for both in-game and chat audio

It's Not All Good

Controller Update Required

In most cases, before you can use the Stereo Headset Adapter by itself or in combination with the Xbox One Stereo Headset, you'll need to update your controller. Follow the update instructions bundled with the adapter, or visit http://support.xbox.com/en-US/xbox-one/accessories/update-controller-for-stereo-headset-adapter for more detailed information. You'll need to do this update on each controller that will make use of the adapter.

Three of the better officially licensed headphone options are the Polk Audio 4Shot and the Turtle Beach Ear Force XO SEVEN and FOUR. The wireless Polk Audio 4Shot comes in a variety of colors, features a retractable boom microphone for chat, and also works with other devices, like tablets, smartphones, and computers. The two Turtle Beach options have a similar feature set as the 4Shot, though they have removable boom microphones and only come in black. Although the FOUR's audio capabilities are not quite as immersive as the 4Shot or SEVEN, it's approximately $50 cheaper and still sports a nice range of features and an impressive 15 hours of battery life.

The Turtle Beach Ear Force XO FOUR is a quality headset that is less expensive than other licensed options

In terms of speaker systems, there are literally dozens of quality options for every budget and desire in a wide range of configurations. Although there is no particular need to go with an officially licensed speaker, the Polk N1 SurroundBar—available in both black and white—is a single, compact unit with full-range Dolby Digital surround support, four different audio modes, and Bluetooth compatibility so that it can be used with other devices. Although nothing beats having seven real speakers and a subwoofer, for those who don't want to deal with the clutter (or expense), the Polk N1 SurroundBar is a fine alternative.

Networking Enhancements

Thanks to the Xbox One's Gigabit networking port, the ideal scenario for making the fastest network connection is always to run an Ethernet cable directly from your console to an Ethernet jack, router, or cable or DSL modem. Unfortunately, the reality is most homes are not set up to support a wired connection. If you haven't already, investing in a wireless router that works on the Wireless-N (802.11n) standard and operates on the 5-GHz frequency will give the best wireless performance. Dual-band routers offer more flexibility, operating in the 2.4-GHz band for longer range and to support older devices, as well as the 5-GHz band for less interference. Although the Xbox One does not support the newest wireless standard, 802.11ac, many such routers do have other useful features, such as signal targeting that can help boost overall performance.

Top-of-the-line wireless routers like the ASUS (RT-AC68) Wireless-AC1900 Dual-Band Gigabit Router can provide a boost to overall network performance for every device on your network

If you find that environmental factors cause your wireless connection to be sluggish or inconsistent, and you can't run Ethernet cable, you should consider investing in a Powerline AV Network Kit. These easy-to-use devices enable you to create a high-speed network connection anywhere in your home via an adaptor that gets plugged in directly to any electrical wall outlet. One adapter gets plugged in to an electrical outlet near your console, and another adapter gets plugged in to an electrical outlet near your router. Most of these setups allow several additional adapters to be added to the mix for other devices that also have a networking port, and some adapters even have multiple input ports. Many quality brands are available, including from Linksys (Powerline), Actiontec (PWR511K01), NETGEAR (Powerline), and D-Link (PowerLine).

The Linksys Homeplug AV2 Powerline Kit (PLEK500) helps connect devices to your home network via your home's power lines

Security Locks

If you're ever concerned about the security of your Xbox One, say if it's in a dorm room or some other public location, your console's lock port has you covered. Known popularly as a laptop (or notebook) security cable, these handy devices are usually nothing more than some type of reinforced cable with either a key or combination lock attached, which snaps into the Xbox One's lock port. The cable is then secured to some type of heavy, reinforced structure, like a table leg. Kensington, which originally designed this type of antitheft system (Kensington Security Slot and Lock), and Sendt make some of the more popular and best-reviewed devices.

Sendt's Notebook/ Laptop Combination Lock Security Cable is one of many quality options for securing your console

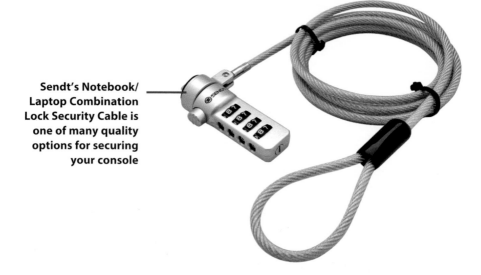

Kinect Accessories

Now that Kinect is such an integral part of the Xbox experience, it's only natural that it too has room for improvement in less-than-ideal situations. For instance, if you have a projector screen or otherwise have nowhere to safely place your Kinect sensor, you might want to try a tripod with a camera mount. Although a standard tripod will work just fine, Foamy Lizard's Kinect Floor Stand for Xbox One is purposely built to an ideal 2-foot height.

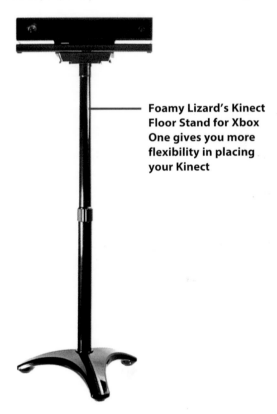

Foamy Lizard's Kinect Floor Stand for Xbox One gives you more flexibility in placing your Kinect

A more direct solution is the PDP Kinect TV Mount, which enables you to securely mount the Kinect to the top of most flat-panel televisions. Its telescoping arm accommodates most TV widths, plus it even comes with a privacy cover that blocks Kinect's cameras for times when you want to be absolutely certain of your privacy.

Similarly, if you'd prefer to mount your Kinect securely to a wall, Foamy Lizard and LETECK both make wall mounts, with the latter also supporting a second configuration—television placement—just like PDP's device. Foamy Lizard also sells a privacy shield by itself.

Learn about the wide range of gaming options on the Xbox One

Games
FEATURED

NEW RELEASES

Forza Motorsport 5
Get inside today's hottest cars

Assassin's Creed IV: Black Flag

Need for Speed Rivals

Search games

Use a code

Call of Duty: Ghosts
Explore this near-future shooter

Madden NFL 25
Get ready for the big game

MACHINIMA

Snap Wingman help videos

ASSASSIN'S CREED IV BLACK FLAG
GAME YEAR
Buy Now
ADVERTISEMENT

Learn about advanced gaming features, including recording gameplay and snapping help videos

In this chapter, you learn about gaming and game-related activities on your Xbox One console and how to take the experience to the next level.

→ Coming to Grips with the Basics

→ Installing and Uninstalling Games and Apps

→ Managing Game Saves in the Cloud

→ Buying Add-ons and DLC with Tokens

→ Referencing Machinima

→ Working with Game DVR, Upload, and Upload Studio

→ Streaming with Twitch

→ Checking Out Some Games

Getting Your Game On

Although your Xbox One offers a tremendous all-around home entertainment center experience, its greatest strength and selling point is its capability to serve up state-of-the-art games. Of course, as with most of its other functionality, the Xbox One does a lot more than just let you play the games. It also lets you record and upload clips of your greatest achievements, lets you reference walk-throughs for those times when you're stuck, and even helps you get into shape with its selection of fitness apps and games. The Xbox One truly redefines what it means to get your game on and this chapter tells you all about it.

Coming to Grips with the Basics

Whether you buy a game on a retail disc or a digital download, every game needs to be installed to your Xbox One's hard drive before you can play it. Fortunately, as long as you have sufficient space on the hard drive, this installation process is automatic and seamless. In most cases, you can even start playing before the whole install is finished.

Retail games that come on disc are available from a wide range of online and physical stores. Digital games, however, are only available from the Games section of the Xbox One Store. You can access the Store from the Home screen and select the Games tile, or say, "Xbox, go to Store, Games," if you want to use Kinect.

Access the Games store from the Store section of the Home screen

Say, "Xbox, Bing," if you'd like to search the Store via Kinect with your voice

The Games store is broken up into 10 sections: Featured; Search Games, Use a Code, and Advertisement; New Releases; Add-ons; Top Games Right Now; Popular Games; Recommended for You; New Game Demos; Top Selling; and Top Rated.

Scroll right to see more Games store categories

With the exceptions of options like Use a Code and Advertisement, these categories are just different ways of sorting the available game library. Select the Ellipsis (three dots) for the full listing in a particular category.

Search Games is another way to search for a particular game outside of using your voice. Use a Code is the usual way of redeeming codes. Advertisement is just that, a commercial that is likely targeted to the male, 18–49 demographic.

New Game Demos lists the latest of the available game demos, which is a great way to try a game for free before you decide if you want to buy. Add-ons lists all of the available game add-ons, like new levels, weapons, or skins (visuals). Adds-ons is itself broken down into additional categories, including Featured, New Releases, and Popular Add-ons.

Scroll right for more categories under Game Add-Ons

Select for the full list in the category

After you select a game from the Store, you see its summary screen. The first section of the game summary screen consists of the following elements:

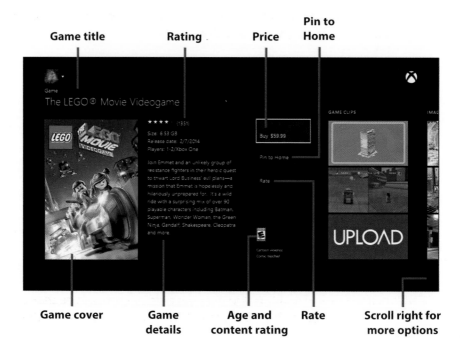

Game title   Rating   Price   Pin to Home

Game cover   Game details   Age and content rating   Rate   Scroll right for more options

- **Game title**—The full name of the game.

- **Game cover**—The official cover art for the game.

- **Rating**—The number of stars, which indicates the average rating given by the number of players shown in the parentheses. The ratings are based on a five-star system, from lowest (one star) to highest (five stars). The more stars, the better the game (based on the reviewers' opinions).

- **Game details**—The amount of space the game takes on the hard drive, the initial release date, and how many local and online players the game supports.

- **Price**—The purchase price for the game, which could be listed as Free for a demo. Selecting this option initiates the transaction if it's a purchase, or prompts you to start the download if it's a demo.

- **Pin to Home**—An option that allows you to pin the game's icon to the Home screen.

- **Rate**—An option that allows you to contribute your own rating for the game between one (worst) and five (best) stars.

- **Age and content rating**—The rating from the Entertainment Software Rating Board (ESRB). See the "Checking Out Some Games" section later in this chapter for more information on the ESRB.

The other categories on the game summary screen are Game Clips, Images, Featured Challenge, You May Also Like, More Details, and Terms of Use. Game Clips shows the latest user clips (videos) saved and shared with Game DVR and Upload Studio (see the "Working with Game DVR, Upload, and Upload Studio" section later in this chapter for more information). Images shows stills (screenshots) from the game. Featured Challenge shows the latest timed special challenge and all of the other possible in-game achievements (see the "Earning Achievements for Games and Media" section in Chapter 3, "Examining Xbox Live," for more information on achievements). You May Also Like is a list of related games. More Details lists the Developer, Publisher, Genre, and additional multiplayer details. Terms of Use shows the Xbox Live Terms of Use, Xbox Live Code of Conduct, and Xbox Live Privacy & Cookies Statement.

>>>Go Further

WANT ACCESS TO EVEN MORE GAMES?

Besides the wide selection of downloadable and retail games, there's actually one more category of gaming possible on the Xbox One. Thanks to the power of the Internet Explorer browser app (see Chapter 10, "Surfing with Internet Explorer") and its support for HTML5, your Xbox One can play web games that have controller support. Although many of these titles are fairly simple diversions, most are also free to play, so they're worth checking out at least once to see if you can find a favorite or two. Go to http://playboxie.com/ and select the Xbox One tile for a list of supported games.

Installing and Uninstalling Games and Apps

Whether purchased on disc or downloaded from the Games store, every game (and downloaded app) gets installed to the Xbox One's 500GB hard drive. Although that sounds like a lot of space, only about 360GB of that is available for storing games and any of their add-ons or expansions. Even that might still sound like a lot—after all, the original Xbox 360's hard drive had a mere 20GB of storage. But with some of the bigger games taking up 40GB or more, suddenly all that available space can go away in a hurry, particularly as your game and app library grows. Luckily, what gets installed on the hard drive is just as easy to uninstall, making room for new games or apps. Of course, as long as you have the disc or are logged in to your account, you can reinstall a game (or app) at any time.

It's Not All Good

What About External Hard Drives?

As of press time, Microsoft has remained mum on the possibility of using USB flash or hard drives with the Xbox One for expanded game storage, simply stating "…this functionality *may* be added later."

Managing Installs

To see how much hard drive space you have, go to My Games & Apps. Available space is listed in the lower-left corner both in terms of GB free and percentage of the available space used.

When you insert a disc or begin a download, installation begins immediately unless there are other installation requests ahead of it in the Queue. You can manage the Queue from My Games & Apps.

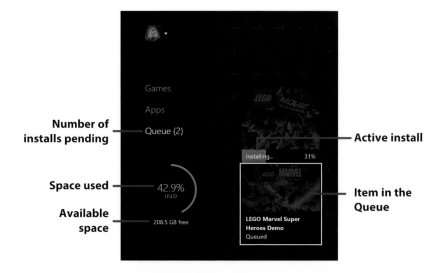

Number of installs pending

Space used

Available space

Active install

Item in the Queue

Queued items can be given installation priority by selecting the item and then pressing the Menu button on the controller. Selecting Install Now moves the item to the top of the Queue. Press the Menu button again to exit.

To uninstall an item, select Games or Apps, respectively, from My Games & Apps. Select the item in the list of installed items and press the Menu button. Select Uninstall.

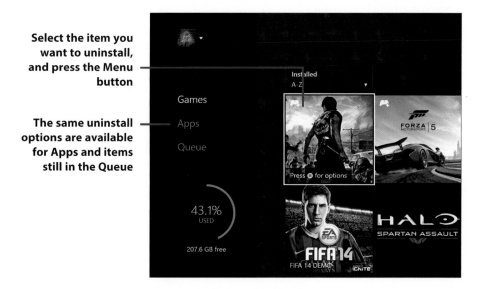

Select the item you want to uninstall, and press the Menu button

The same uninstall options are available for Apps and items still in the Queue

Playing as You Install a Game

Games and demos are installed incrementally. As a result, once a sufficient portion of the game or demo is installed, you can start playing it even before it's complete. Just look for the words Ready to Start on the game's tile.

If you see Ready to Start, you can begin playing before installation is complete — Ready to start   20% — **Press the Menu button to pause or cancel the installation**

The percentage required to start playing varies by title and, even when you can launch a title that's not fully installed, not all features are immediately available.

What About Preloading Games?

Microsoft has promised a feature where if a game is purchased digitally prior to its official release, you will be able to download the game before it's officially available. The game will then be available for play after 12:01 a.m. PST on its release date. Once fully implemented, this will be another great time-saving feature, particularly for the larger downloadable games.

Managing Game Saves in the Cloud

As long as you're connected to Xbox Live, your saved games are automatically stored in the cloud in addition to the data stored on your console. This means that if you sign in to a different Xbox One console, your saves are accessible there and continue to be automatically saved to the cloud, allowing you to pick up right where you left off wherever you happen to log in.

Delete a Saved Game

Although the cloud saving process is automatic, there might be situations where you'll want to delete saves you no longer need. To delete these saves, do the following:

1. From the Home screen, select My Games & Apps.

2. Highlight the game with the save data you want to delete and press the Menu button on the controller.

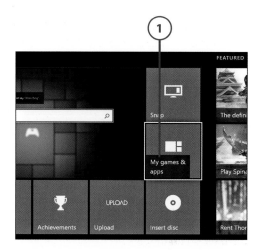

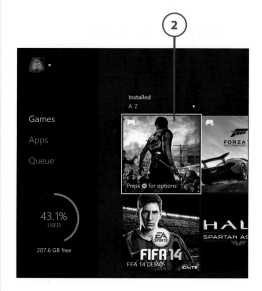

3. Select Manage Game.

4. Scroll to the right to highlight the saved data under Saved Data. Press the A button on your controller.

5. You are presented with three options:

    - **Delete from Console**—Removes the local copy of your saved data on the current console's hard drive. The cloud data remains.

    - **Delete Everywhere**—Removes both the local copy of your saved data and the cloud data. The saved game information is no longer available anywhere.

    - **Cancel**—Cancels the operation, leaving all of your saved data intact.

Buying Add-ons and DLC with Tokens

Tokens are a type of currency for select titles that are typically purchased with real money from the Add-ons section of the Games store. Tokens can be used to purchase various in-game add-ons, downloadable content (DLC), and upgrades, like cars and game accelerators in *Forza Motorsport 5*, although not all games make use of them.

Purchase tokens in a game or app's Add-ons section in the Games store

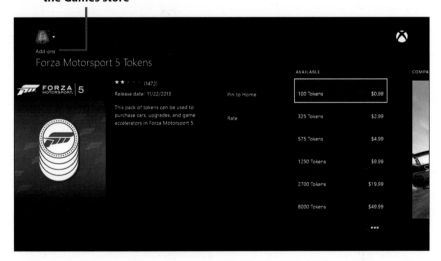

After you redeem tokens for downloadable game content or a game, the content is not automatically installed. These items need to be manually installed from My Games & Apps.

Install an Add-on

To install add-ons or downloadable
game content, do the following:

1. Select the My Games & Apps tile.

2. Highlight the game you have the
   new content for.

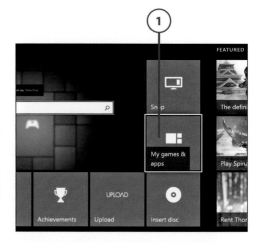

3. Press the Menu button and select Manage Game.

4. Scroll right and select an item in the Ready to Install section. Press the A button on your controller.

5. Highlight Install, then press the A button on your controller to begin installation.

Referencing Machinima

Machinima, a portmanteau of *machine* and *cinema*, is defined as the art of creating animated videos in real-time virtual game environments. Machinima.com is a gaming and media streaming website that specializes in hosting such videos. The Machinima app for Xbox One is your portal to the features of the website, including watching Machinima shows, finding your favorite Machinima partners, and watching gameplay videos for the games you play.

If you don't already have Machinima listed in your apps, go to the Apps section of the Store, or do a Bing search, to find and install it.

**Press the A button to
install the app**

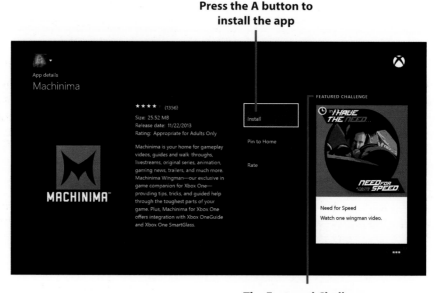

**The Featured Challenge
and Leaderboard are
located to the right**

Once installed, the full breadth of Machinima features becomes available after the app is launched.

**Search for a video of your
favorite game**

**Scroll right to see a variety of
categories and featured videos**

Perhaps the best feature of the Machinima app on Xbox One is how it works with Snap. When you're playing a game, simply say "Xbox, Snap Machinima" to make it a companion app in Snap mode. The app automatically recognizes the game you're playing and, if available, takes you to relevant gameplay videos.

If you're stuck in a particular section of a game or just want to learn how to play better, this is a great way to locate walk-throughs or simply see how others play the game.

**Many Xbox One games have Machinima video
collections that you can reference as you play**

**Choose the Collection and Video
you'd like to see, and then select Play**

>>>Go Further

WHY REGISTER WITH MACHINIMA?

Although you can use Machinima without having to register, signing in provides for a more customized experience. This includes adding content to your Queue, favoriting videos, and sharing your own videos. You can register at the Machinima website (www.machinima.com) or directly within the app using the Login Button from the App Menu. This launches the Internet Explorer app where you need to sign in to Facebook. Once that happens, you will receive confirmation that you registered in the application.

Working with Game DVR, Upload, and Upload Studio

You might have seen Microsoft promote a feature of Xbox One called Game DVR, a tool that enables you to record the best moments in your games. Some clips, like when you earn an achievement or beat a particularly tricky area, are automatically recorded. Others you can choose to record yourself.

You can then access and work with these clips from the Upload app, which allows you to share any of these clips with friends or browse clips that others upload. Upload Studio, or Upload as it appears on the app tile, provides a richer set of options for editing and customizing your clips.

So, whereas Game DVR enables you to capture gameplay video clips, it's with Upload Studio that you do your editing and sharing of them. Recordings are set at a resolution of 720p and run at 30 frames per second.

Besides automatic recordings, you can at any time say, "Xbox, record that" to immediately capture the last 30 seconds of gameplay. If you want longer recordings, you can snap the Game DVR app and set your own interval of up to 5 minutes in length.

Record with Game DVR

To snap the Game DVR app to make recordings of a length of your choosing, start the game you want to record and do the following:

1. Say "Xbox, Snap Game DVR."

    Alternately, if Kinect is off, return to the Home screen by pressing the Xbox button on your controller. Select Game DVR from My Games & Apps.

2. Select a recording option:

    - **End Clip Now**—Creates a video of the previous 30 seconds, 45 seconds, 1 minute, 3 minutes, or 5 minutes of gameplay, depending upon your selection

    - **Start New Clip**—Records up to the next 5 minutes of what you're about to do in the game

    - **Show My Clips**—Goes to Upload Studio to see your previously recorded clips

After you've recorded a clip, a notification pops up indicating its success. You can then leave the recording as an unsaved, temporary Game DVR clip. To keep a clip from expiring, save the clip in the Upload app or edit the clip in Upload Studio.

Upload a Clip

The Upload app shows the most recent clips you recorded with Game DVR and the clips that others have uploaded and shared. Select the Upload tile from My Games & Apps to start the app.

Scroll right for more options

Inside the Upload app, you'll note that most selections are categories of clips others have uploaded, including those clips with added Kinect video or audio commentary. Selecting Upload Studio takes you to the Upload Studio app, while selecting My Clips brings you to both your temporary and saved clips.

A temporary, unsaved clip   **Indicates a saved clip**

Select to play all of your clips

Select to go back

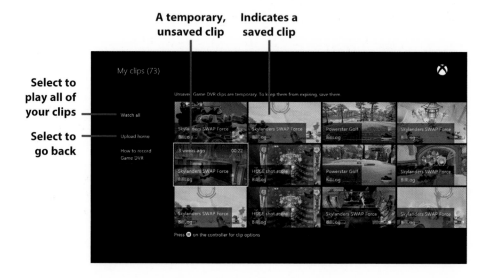

When you select My Clips, you see all of your temporary and saved clips. If you highlight a clip and press the Menu button, you have the option to save or edit the clip, play the game from which it was generated, or delete the clip. A white check mark on a green background in the upper-right corner of the clip indicates a saved clip. Temporary clips have no check mark.

Using Upload Studio

The Upload Studio app is a utility for editing and customizing video clips. You can work from Game DVR clips captured with Upload, or you can record video or audio commentary about your clips using Kinect. You can then edit and customize your clips.

Unlike Upload, Upload Studio is not installed by default. You can install Upload Studio by going to the Apps section of the Store or by doing a Bing search for "Upload Studio." Select Install to install Upload Studio.

To edit the gameplay videos that you've recorded with the Game DVR feature of Upload in Upload Studio, select Start Editing after Upload Studio starts.

**Overview of a typical workflow:
Record, Edit, and Share**

**Select to
start editing**

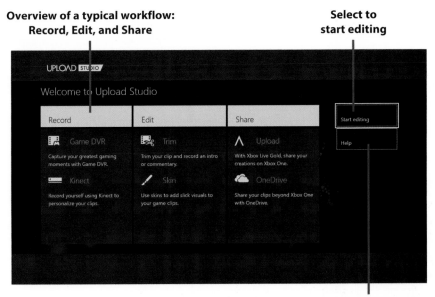

**Provides helpful
descriptions for Upload
Studio's features**

After selecting Start Editing, the first step is to choose a template, which defines the overall structure of your video. The following options are available to help you determine how many clips you'll use and how you'll fit them together:

Use templates to determine what kind of clip you want to make

- **Just Trim**—Trim, or remove, some length of video. This is the simplest form of editing.

- **Picture-in-Picture**—Combine two Game DVR or Kinect recordings to run simultaneously in the same video. You can choose which of the two videos is the primary video.

- **Bookend**—String three clips together.

- **Multi-clip**—String five clips together.

Each of the four template options has similar editing options once selected. We use the Picture-in-Picture template here as a representative example:

Add clips

Second clip
segment

Customize

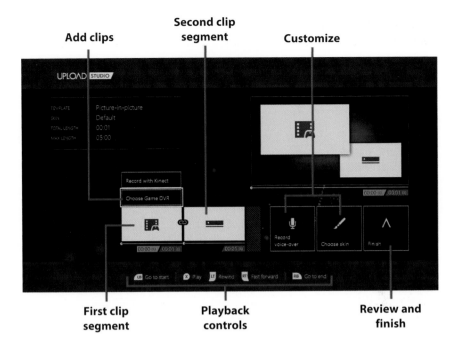

First clip
segment

Playback
controls

Review and
finish

- **Add clips**—Select a clip segment, then select either Record with Kinect to create a new recording with Kinect or Choose Game DVR to use existing clips. Repeat this process for all remaining clip segments.

- **Customize**—After all of the clips have been added, you can optionally Record Voice-over or Choose Skin. Record Voice-over lets you narrate your video, whereas Choose Skin lets you add a theme to your video.

- **Review and finish**—Review your video using the playback controls at the bottom of the screen. When you're happy with your creation, select Finish to finalize your edits to the clip.

It's Not All Good

Watch the Language!

All clips are screened for violations of the Xbox Live Code of Conduct. This means any foul or offensive material is subject to censure and may result in your Xbox Live privileges being suspended or revoked. Refer to www.xbox.com/en-US/legal/codeofconduct for the list of do's and don'ts.

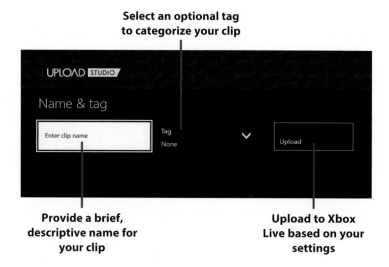

**Select an optional tag
to categorize your clip**

**Provide a brief,
descriptive name for
your clip**

**Upload to Xbox
Live based on your
settings**

After you select Finish, you just need to provide a name and tag (category), then upload your clip. Once you select Upload, Xbox One renders your clip. Depending upon whether you selected Allow or Block under Privacy & Family Safety, Customize, or Share Game Clips determines whether your uploaded clips are visible to all Xbox Live users (refer to "Breaking Down the Settings Screen" in Chapter 2, "Navigating Your Xbox One's Dashboard and Settings," for more information on Settings). Refer to "Share Files" in Chapter 9, "Managing Files with OneDrive," for information on manually sharing your clips to YouTube, Facebook, Twitter, and other services.

Streaming with Twitch

An alternative to recording and editing your gameplay is Twitch, which is a live streaming video platform. Think of it as online TV, only with video games. And absolutely anyone can broadcast on it without first being greenlit by a network guy in a snazzy suit. Pretty cool!

Using the Twitch app on Xbox One, you can not only watch game broadcasts from others, but also record your own gameplay and optional picture-in-picture commentary by simply saying, "Xbox, broadcast."

Of course, Twitch is also great for some of the same types of things that Machinima is, including how it works with Snap. When you're playing a game, say "Xbox, Snap Twitch" to make it a companion app in Snap mode. From there, you can select the appropriate game video to see how others have played through a particular section that you're stuck on or simply to see some general techniques others use when they play.

Install Twitch

The Twitch app must be installed before use. To install Twitch, do the following:

1. Go to Twitch's App details screen either from the Apps section of the Xbox Store, by using Bing to search for it, or by saying, "Xbox, go to Twitch" or "Xbox, broadcast."

2. Select Get It FREE and then Confirm, when prompted.

3. After it's installed, select Launch. You're now at the Twitch home screen.

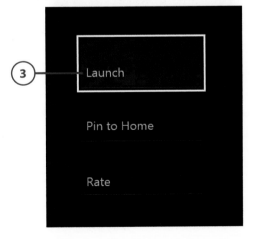

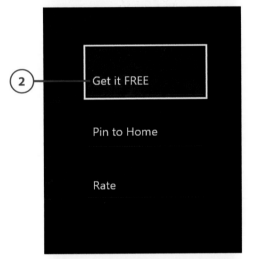

>>>Go Further

WHAT TO DO IN TWITCH

From the Twitch home screen, you can select the Search option or browse through one of several categories to watch specific videos. You'll also be able to expand your Friends list by viewing the gamer card of anyone streaming from an Xbox One and then following them. Best of all, of course, you can broadcast your own videos, but only after you log in.

Log In to Twitch

To log in to Twitch and get started doing some of your own broadcasting, do the following:

1. Select Log In.

2. Make a note of the six-digit code on your screen and use a Web browser to go to http://twitch.tv/activate.

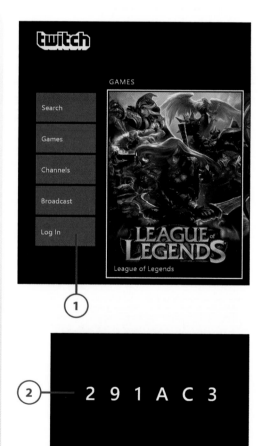

3. Click on the Sign Up tab and enter the requested information.

4. Click on the Sign Up button.

5. Enter the six-digit code from step 2 and click the Activate button.

6. Your Xbox One Gamertag is now linked to your Twitch account. The Log In button on your Xbox One is now your Twitch account username.

Broadcasting with Twitch

After you complete the one-time setup of a Twitch account, you can begin live streaming a game of your choice at any point while playing it by saying, "Xbox, broadcast." Kinect enables you to include a picture-in-picture video feed and audio commentary along with the game broadcast. Although use of Kinect and its microphone is optional, it can make your broadcast more interesting than just streaming the gameplay.

Checking Out Some Games

There are two types of Xbox One games: retail and digital only. Retail games come on physical discs available for purchase from various retail outlets and can usually also be downloaded from the Games section of the Xbox Store on the same date as the disc version (exceptions are generally games like *Skylanders: SWAP Force* that require special hardware add-ons). Digital-only games can be downloaded only from the Games section of the Xbox Store.

Optional game add-ons and expansions are also only available digitally for download. With more than 30 retail and digital-only games released in the Xbox One's first 4 months on the market and more games being added on nearly a weekly basis, picking just the right game can be an intimidating proposition. Luckily, this ever-growing volume of games also means that every player type, preference, and need can be satisfied. How do you pick just the right game, though?

One of the best ways to find out if you like a game is to actually play it, either at a store kiosk, at a friend's house, or through a demo. Unfortunately, the first two options may not be options at all, and, frustratingly, not every game has a demo available for download.

If you have no way to try before you buy, then the next best option is to arm yourself with as much information as possible. Watch game clips from your fellow gamers on your Xbox One or elsewhere online like YouTube or Twitch, ask friends and family on social networks, and read reviews from both professional game websites and from consumers who leave feedback at your favorite retail websites. Always remember, though, that reviews are not the be-all and end-all because, ultimately, only you know what you like.

There is, however, one way to stack the review odds in your favor, and that's with Metacritic (www.metacritic.com). The Metacritic website aggregates music, TV, movie, and game reviews from leading critics. The site uses weighted averages to convert these reviews into percentages between 0 (worst) and 100 (best), referred to as Metascore. Similarly, Metacritic visitors can provide their own, often harsher and sometimes far less informed, ratings, between 0 (worst) and 10 (best), referred to as User Scores. Links to individual reviews, game details and credits, and trailers and videos are also provided. Whenever available, both the latest Metascore and User Scores for each of the retail and digital-only games (see the following sections) is provided.

What Does the Metascore Really Mean?

Although Metacritic's User Scores are provided in a straightforward, 10-point basis, what about the Metascore percentages? Metacritic lists 0–19 as Overwhelming Dislike, 20–49 as Generally Unfavorable, 50–74 as Mixed or Average, 75–89 as Generally Favorable, and 90–100 as Universal Acclaim. However, Metacritic scores should hardly be considered gospel. A lot of games that individual people love to pieces don't always rate well by the crowd. Metacritic is a useful tool, but it's not a substitute for your own judgment and experience.

Understanding Game Ratings

As you found out in Chapter 2, your Xbox One has privacy and online safety settings that can help you restrict access to movies, TV, music, apps, and games that exceed a particular rating. For games, the rating system determined by the ESRB is used. Even if you don't specifically restrict games with a particular rating in Settings, it still might be important to know what the ratings mean before you make a purchase. The most commonly used ratings are E for Everyone, which means suitable for all ages (Everyone 10+ is recommended for those aged 10 and up); T for Teen, which means 13 and up; and M for Mature, which means recommended for those aged 17 and up. As with other forms of media, retail packaging or digital listings list what subjects or themes are present in the game, such as blood, sexual themes, strong language, use of drugs, and violence.

Perusing Retail Games

Retail games, whether bought in disc form from a store or downloaded digitally are typically releases that have higher production values or are larger in scope than their digital-only counterparts. Still, quality varies greatly from game to game and there are plenty of examples out there of high-priced dogs and low-budget gems. The difference between a title getting a retail release versus a digital-only release might come down to nothing more than logistics. In fact, there are even situations where certain retail games, like *Zoo Tycoon*, only get released at a single retail outlet for a set period of time (in this case, Walmart), making a digital purchase seem like the only option for those not aware of the exclusivity window.

Now, let's take a look at some of the Xbox One retail games that just might be worth your time.

Angry Birds Star Wars

- **Developer:** Extient

- **Publisher:** Activision

- **Genre:** Puzzle, strategy

- **Players:** 1–4

- **Learning curve:** Low

- **Supported features:** Kinect

- **ESRB rating:** Everyone

The classic mobile game where you slingshot birds at evil, egg-stealing pigs gets a nice Xbox One entry, complete with *Star Wars* theme and alternating co-op and multiplayer. Although the optional Kinect controls are overly finicky, playing with the controller is just as satisfying as it is with a touch screen. Unfortunately, beyond the multiplayer modes and biweekly challenge objectives, there's not much value over the significantly less-expensive mobile versions of the game.

Assassin's Creed IV: Black Flag

- **Developer:** Ubisoft

- **Publisher:** Ubisoft

- **Genre:** Action-adventure, open world, stealth

- **Players:** 1, online multiplayer 2–8

- **Learning curve:** High
- **Supported features:** Kinect, SmartGlass, companion app
- **ESRB rating:** Mature

Set in the eighteenth century Caribbean, this game tasks you with the role of notorious pirate Edward Kenway in the "Golden Age of Piracy," as you explore and fight from a third-person perspective on both sea and land in open world settings. The audiovisual presentation delights and plenty of side quests and online multiplayer options add to the already expansive main game. If you can get a grasp on the sometimes overwhelming controls and in-game options, there's no denying that *Assassin's Creed IV: Black Flag* provides a tremendous gameplay experience, which is extended through clever use of SmartGlass and a companion mobile app.

Battlefield 4

- **Developer:** DICE
- **Publisher:** Electronic Arts
- **Genre:** First-person shooter
- **Players:** 1, online multiplayer 4–64
- **Learning curve:** High
- **Supported features:** Kinect, SmartGlass
- **ESRB rating:** Mature

Set in a near-future 2020 where the United States, Russia, and China are at the brink of war, you take the role of Sgt Daniel "Reck" Recker, a member of a U.S. special operations squad call-signed "Tombstone." In the single-player campaign, you both engage enemy targets directly and command your squadmates to do the same as you gain valuable experience and weapons for use in the real meat of the game, online multiplayer. Although the game has received its fair share of criticism for numerous game-stopping bugs, the developer has promised fixes that should continue to improve the game's playability over time.

Call of Duty: Ghosts

- **Developer:** Infinity Ward
- **Publisher:** Activision
- **Genre:** First-person shooter
- **Players:** 1–2, online multiplayer 2–18
- **Learning curve:** High
- **Supported features:** Kinect
- **ESRB rating:** Mature

In the single-player campaign, you take the role of U.S. Sgt Logan Walker and several other characters in an alternate timeline that follows the nuclear destruction of the Middle East. As with *Battlefield 4*, *Call of Duty: Ghosts* shines in multiplayer, with well over a dozen different modes, including co-op.

Dead Rising 3

- **Developer:** Capcom Vancouver
- **Publisher:** Microsoft Studios
- **Genre:** Survival horror
- **Players:** 1, online multiplayer 2
- **Learning curve:** Medium
- **Supported features:** Kinect, SmartGlass
- **ESRB rating:** Mature

Assume the role of mechanic Nick Ramos who is trapped in a city overrun by a zombie outbreak. Use Nick's skills to pick up, craft, and utilize all kinds of crazy weapons and vehicles to battle the hordes of screen-filling zombies as you try to make an escape. Thanks to Kinect, zombies can hear your shouts, while SmartGlass functionality can be used to locate specific items and places, set waypoints for mission objectives, and play exclusive missions. Several online cooperative play modes add to the fun.

FIFA 14

- **Developer:** EA Canada
- **Publisher:** Electronic Arts
- **Genre:** Sports
- **Players:** 1–4, online multiplayer 2–22
- **Learning curve:** Medium
- **Supported features:** None
- **ESRB rating:** Everyone

With impressive audiovisuals and an uncanny knack for simulating the movements and performance of real-world players, *FIFA 14* continues the tradition of excellence for one of Electronic Arts' most consistent annual sports game releases. Although it's fun just to kick the ball around, this game is at its best when players dig deep and try to play like the professionals do.

Forza Motorsport 5

- **Developer:** Turn 10 Studios
- **Publisher:** Microsoft Studios
- **Genre:** Racing
- **Players:** 1–2, online multiplayer 1–16
- **Learning curve:** Medium

- **Supported features:** Kinect, SmartGlass, Force feedback wheel
- **ESRB rating:** Everyone

With hundreds of painstakingly modeled cars from more than 50 manufacturers and more than a dozen authentic racing circuits to choose from, *Forza Motorsport 5* doesn't skimp on the details. The stunning audiovisuals are complemented by a sophisticated racing engine that requires real skill to master. Perhaps the game's most intriguing feature is its use of *Drivatar* technology, which learns about and then simulates both how you and your online friends drive, creating an even more realistic competitive racing environment.

Just Dance 2014

- **Developer:** Ubisoft Milan
- **Publisher:** Ubisoft
- **Genre:** Rhythm
- **Players:** 1–6
- **Learning curve:** Low
- **Supported features:** Kinect (required), SmartGlass
- **ESRB rating:** Everyone

Featuring more than 40 dance tracks, *Just Dance 2014* uses the power of Kinect to score how well you and up to five family members or friends are following the onscreen dance moves. Luckily, the game is designed for fun first and as such is quite forgiving for those born with two left feet.

LEGO Marvel Super Heroes

- **Developer:** TT Games
- **Publisher:** Warner Bros. Interactive Entertainment
- **Genre:** Action-adventure
- **Players:** 1–2
- **Learning curve:** Low
- **Supported features:** None
- **ESRB rating:** Everyone

One or two players take control of an amazing array of iconic Marvel super heroes like Spider-Man and the Hulk to battle villains and solve simple puzzles in a LEGO universe. It's a great action game in a series known for having fun with its plastic brick-based environments.

Madden NFL 25

- **Developer:** EA Tiburon

- **Publisher:** Electronic Arts

- **Genre:** Sports

- **Players:** 1–4, online multiplayer 2–6

- **Learning curve:** Medium

- **Supported features:** SmartGlass

- **ESRB rating:** Everyone

Improved artificial intelligence and crisper audiovisuals make this release one of the best entries yet in the long-running annual game series. Although not without its flaws, if you like real NFL football, it's the only game in town.

NBA 2K14

- **Developer:** Visual Concepts Entertainment

- **Publisher:** 2K

- **Genre:** Sports

- **Players:** 1–4, online multiplayer 2–10

- **Learning curve:** Medium

- **Supported features:** None

- **ESRB rating:** Everyone

With crisp gameplay and even crisper visuals, *NBA 2K14* delivers a professional basketball experience unlike any other. Although it has a relatively high learning curve typical of today's sports games, it's worth the effort to experience all the game has to offer. Take a pass on Electronic Arts' *NBA Live 14*, which has nowhere near the same polish as 2K's game.

Need for Speed: Rivals

- **Developer:** Ghost Games
- **Publisher:** Electronic Arts
- **Genre:** Racing
- **Players:** 1, online multiplayer 2–6
- **Learning curve:** Low
- **Supported features:** None
- **ESRB rating:** Everyone (10+)

In stark contrast to *Forza Motorsport 5*'s impeccable racing simulation, *Need for Speed: Rivals* goes for a less-intimidating, more action-packed experience. Luckily, the audiovisuals and controls are similarly top notch and make fine companions to the fun, over-the-top gameplay.

Plants vs. Zombies: Garden Warfare

- **Developer:** PopCap Games Vancouver
- **Publisher:** Electronic Arts
- **Genre:** Third-person shooter
- **Players:** 1–2, online multiplayer 1–26
- **Learning curve:** Low
- **Supported features:** SmartGlass
- **ESRB rating:** Everyone (10+)

Plants vs. Zombies: Garden Warfare takes the classic strategy game into a fresh, action-packed direction, all while staying true to the original game's quirky, lighthearted personality. Lots of multiplayer and other game modes make this third-person shooter (with a touch of strategy) a title you'll want to come back to time and again.

Rayman Legends

- **Developer:** Ubisoft Montpellier

- **Publisher:** Ubisoft

- **Genre:** Platformer

- **Players:** 1–4

- **Learning curve:** Low

- **Supported features:** None

- **ESRB rating:** Everyone (10+)

Rayman Legends is one of the best platformers of all time. With lushly illustrated visuals, quirky characters, and imaginative gameplay, it's a delight for gamers of all ages. Supporting up to four simultaneous players, it makes a great party game.

Ryse: Son of Rome

- **Developer:** Crytek

- **Publisher:** Microsoft Studios

- **Genre:** Action-adventure

- **Players:** 1, online multiplayer 1–2

- **Learning curve:** Low

- **Supported features:** Kinect, SmartGlass

- **ESRB rating:** Mature

As soldier Marius Titus, conduct a campaign to avenge the death of your family and seek to restore the honor of Rome in this action-packed tale of revenge, betrayal, and divine intervention. A Gladiator mode is available for those players who want to get straight to the action.

Skylanders: SWAP Force

- **Developer:** Vicarious Visions

- **Publisher:** Activision

- **Genre:** Platformer

- **Players:** 1–2

- **Learning curve:** Low

- **Supported features:** None

- **ESRB rating:** Everyone (10+)

Use a USB-powered portal to bring proprietary action figures (some with swappable top and bottom halves) into the game world. Specific character types—some of which are sold separately—are required to unlock all areas of the game. The cooperative multiplayer and varied environments are fun, but be prepared to pay extra for more toys to get the complete experience beyond what's included in the Console Starter Pack.

The LEGO Movie Videogame

- **Developer:** Traveller's Tales

- **Publisher:** Warner Bros. Interactive

- **Genre:** Action-adventure

- **Players:** 1–2

- **Learning curve:** Low

- **Supported features:** None

- **ESRB rating:** Everyone (10+)

Take the role of Emmet, an ordinary, rules-following, perfectly average LEGO minifigure who is mistakenly identified as the most extraordinary individual who is key to saving the world. An injection of humor straight from the movie helps elevate what would otherwise be another solid, if somewhat uninspiring, entry in the long-running LEGO games series.

Thief

- **Developer:** Eidos Montreal
- **Publisher:** Square Enix
- **Genre:** Stealth
- **Players:** 1
- **Learning curve:** Medium
- **Supported features:** None
- **ESRB rating:** Mature

In this fourth entry in the cult classic series, control master thief Garrett as he returns to his hometown and attempts to shift the balance of power between rich and poor. Stealth is prized over violence as Garrett makes use of his environment to try to successfully evade detection, while also accomplishing his objectives.

Titanfall

- **Developer:** Respawn Entertainment
- **Publisher:** Electronic Arts
- **Genre:** First-person shooter
- **Players:** Online multiplayer, 1–12
- **Learning curve:** Medium
- **Supported features:** SmartGlass
- **ESRB rating:** Mature

Fight in giant, human-piloted robots, or mechs, known as Titans, in intense online-only multiplayer matches. The action also takes place on foot in addition to inside the Titans, with the first-person perspective offering a great sense of scale. This popular game successfully merges the benefits of single-player gaming, like plot, character interaction, and nonplayer characters, into its intense, multiplayer gaming, offering a true next-generation experience.

Tomb Raider: Definitive Edition

- **Developer:** Crystal Dynamics
- **Publisher:** Square Enix
- **Genre:** Action-adventure
- **Players:** 1, online multiplayer 4–8
- **Learning curve:** Low
- **Supported features:** None
- **ESRB rating:** Mature

Experience video game legend Lara Croft's origin story as she develops from a young woman to a hardened adventurer. Although this game debuted to critical acclaim on previous generation consoles, this "Definitive Edition" takes advantage of the Xbox One's power to deliver a more sublime audio-visual experience. Be sure to check out the online multiplayer, a first for the popular series.

Zoo Tycoon

- **Developer:** Frontier Developments Ltd.
- **Publisher:** Microsoft Studio
- **Genre:** Simulation, strategy
- **Players:** 1, online multiplayer 2–4
- **Learning curve:** Low
- **Supported features:** Kinect
- **ESRB rating:** Everyone

In this unique, approachable simulation, build a successful zoo using well over 100 different animals and park components. Use Kinect's voice and motion controls to more seamlessly interact with your zoo animals. Run your zoo alone or with up to four of your friends online.

Zumba Fitness: World Party

- **Developer:** Zoe Mode
- **Publisher:** Majesco Entertainment
- **Genre:** Rhythm
- **Players:** 1–2
- **Learning curve:** Low
- **Supported features:** Kinect
- **ESRB rating:** Everyone

Get fit and have fun by dancing to more than 40 new routines set to both original music and today's top pop hits. Up to two players can dance together with more than 30 different dance styles as Kinect tracks every move.

Perusing Digital-Only Games

Although it's true that digital-only games are initially targeted for exclusive download availability on the Games section of the Xbox Store, occasionally these titles are also bundled together with other digital-only releases on a single retail disc. However, this is not a common practice and if you'd like a digital-only game, it's probably best just to purchase it digitally. This way, any time you want to reinstall or play the game, you'll never need a disc.

Now, let's take a look at some of the Xbox One digital-only games that just might be worth your time.

Crimson Dragon

- **Developer:** Grounding/ LAND HO!
- **Publisher:** Microsoft Studios
- **Genre:** Shooter
- **Players:** 1, online multiplayer 2–3
- **Learning curve:** Low
- **Supported features:** None
- **ESRB rating:** Teen

A spiritual successor to the popular *Panzer Dragoon* series, *Crimson Dragon* tasks players with riding flying dragons and leveling them up as you go. Instead of worrying about flying the dragons, players need to concentrate on shooting the various enemies in a game type known as an "on-rails shooter." Play with up to two other friends online.

Halo: Spartan Assault

- **Developer:** Vanguard Games
- **Publisher:** Microsoft Studios
- **Genre:** Top-down shooter
- **Players:** 1, online multiplayer 1–2
- **Learning curve:** Low
- **Supported features:** None
- **ESRB rating:** Teen

Rather than the usual epic first-person shooter, *Halo: Spartan Assault* changes the classic *Halo* formula into a top-down, third-person shooter based around accomplishing brief mission objectives. Although some players may balk at the scaled-down scope, the beloved *Halo* look and feel remain intact.

Killer Instinct

- **Developer:** Double Helix
- **Publisher:** Microsoft Studios
- **Genre:** Fighting
- **Players:** 1–2, online multiplayer 1–2
- **Learning curve:** Medium
- **Supported features:** None
- **ESRB rating:** Teen

This latest entry in the classic *Killer Instinct* fighting game series was released in a unique manner, for free, with all available game modes, but only one playable character, Jago. Players then have the ability to purchase additional fighters individually. As an alternative, dedicated players can purchase the "Combo Breaker Pack," which provides access to all eight characters, or the "Ultra Edition," which adds additional character accessory packs, costumes, and a playable version of the original 1994 *Killer Instinct* arcade game as *Killer Instinct Classic*.

LocoCycle

- **Developer:** Twisted Pixel

- **Publisher:** Microsoft Studios

- **Genre:** Fighting, racing

- **Players:** 1

- **Learning curve:** Low

- **Supported features:** SmartGlass

- **ESRB rating:** Teen

Long, live-action cutscenes highlight this over-the-top, often funny take on cheesy, big-budget action movies. You control I.R.I.S., a sentient, talking motorcycle who has more than 40 combat moves and speaks 50 languages. Unfortunately for her Spanish-speaking mechanic, Pablo, who she drags around behind her throughout the game, I.R.I.S. is mostly oblivious to the high-stakes events going on around her. The visuals are merely OK and the gameplay not particularly varied, but this quirky title should be a winner for those who find its particular brand of humor appealing.

Max: The Curse of Brotherhood

- **Developer:** Press Play

- **Publisher:** Microsoft Studios

- **Genre:** Platformer

- **Players:** 1

- **Learning curve:** Low

- **Supported features:** None

- **ESRB rating:** Everyone (10+)

Take control of Max as he tries to save his younger brother Felix from the evil forces he inadvertently wished to take him away. Use a magic marker to help Max overcome the challenging otherworldly obstacles on his quest. Although it has its frustrating moments, the platforming and creative elements are imaginative, and the game puts you right back in place to try again when you die.

Peggle 2

- **Developer:** PopCap
- **Publisher:** Electronic Arts
- **Genre:** Puzzle
- **Players:** 1–2, online multiplayer 2–4
- **Learning curve:** Low
- **Supported features:** Kinect
- **ESRB rating:** Everyone

A sequel to the popular multiplatform puzzle game combining elements of pachinko and bagatelle with silly characters and environments, *Peggle 2* tasks its players with skillfully shooting a limited supply of balls at colored pegs to clear its levels. While the sequel amps up the levels, power-ups, and multi-player modes, the new Kinect motion and voice-control features are mostly unnecessary given the precision of the wireless controller.

Powerstar Golf

- **Developer:** Zoe Mode
- **Publisher:** Microsoft Studios
- **Genre:** Sports
- **Players:** 1–4, online multiplayer
- **Learning curve:** Low
- **Supported features:** None
- **ESRB rating:** Everyone

Although not a true simulation, *Powerstar Golf* succeeds in making the sport of golf fun for everyone. With easy-to-understand controls and lots of ways to play and compete, this is a game with lasting appeal.

Strider

- **Developer:** Double Helix Games

- **Publisher:** Capcom

- **Genre:** Platformer, fighting

- **Players:** 1

- **Learning curve:** Low

- **Supported features:** None

- **ESRB Rating:** Everyone (10+)

A modern retelling of the classic arcade and console game, *Strider* places players in control of ninjalike agent, Strider Hiryu. Fight and explore in Kazakh City to ultimately defeat the villainous Grandmaster Meio in a game that emphasizes speed and style.

Xbox Fitness

- **Developer:** Sumo Digital

- **Publisher:** Microsoft Studios

- **Genre:** Fitness

- **Players:** 1

- **Learning curve:** Low

- **Supported features:** Kinect

- **ESRB rating:** Everyone

Using the power of Kinect, exercise along to the world's most famous fitness trainers and workout programs. Kinect maps your muscles to measure exertion, balance, and form, as well as detects microfluctuations in your skin to optically read your heart rate. An onscreen energy meter illustrates your energy utilization, encouraging you to keep pace until each exercise is complete. Compare your Fit Points and scores with your past efforts, friends, and the Xbox Live community at large to stay motivated.

Send messages to other Xbox Live users

Send party and game invitations or both at once

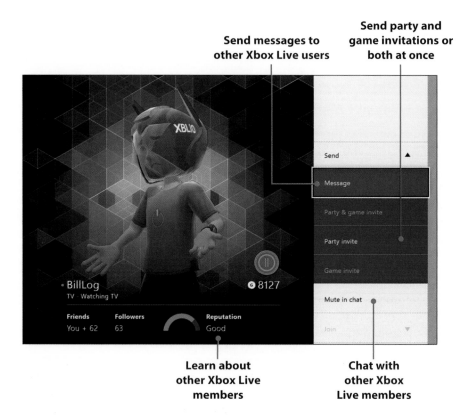

Learn about other Xbox Live members

Chat with other Xbox Live members

In this chapter, you learn how to use your Xbox One console to communicate with your friends via the Friends app, party chat, and Skype.

→ Understanding the Friends App
→ Interacting with Friends
→ Learning About Your Friends
→ Getting the Party Started
→ Keeping In Touch via Skype

Making the Social Connection

It is incredibly easy to use your Xbox One console to communicate with your friends and socialize with them by engaging in activities together, such as playing games or watching movies. Of course, to derive the full benefit of your console as a communications vehicle, you need to have Xbox Live Gold enabled. For more on Xbox Live, turn to Chapter 3, "Examining Xbox Live."

In this chapter, you learn different ways to communicate with your friends via your Xbox One. In addition to examining various Xbox-specific apps, such as the Friends and Party apps, you also review Skype.

Understanding the Friends App

When you access the Social tile from the Home screen, you are brought to the Friends app, from which you can manage and keep tabs on all of your friends or anyone you follow. The Friends app is also accessible from the Apps section of My Games & Apps.

When you access the Friends app, the following options are available to you:

- **All**—Shows all of your friends, breaking out who is currently online.

- **Favorites**—Lists people you've selected as your closest buddies so that you can find them more easily on your Friends list. These people always appear at the top of any friend listings, such as the list of Online friends (if they happen to be online) and the Friends feed.

- **Followers**—Shows people who you follow and who follow you. This can be a good way to keep tabs on acquaintances or even follow celebrities, provided that's something you're into. Individuals following you will become a friend if you add them as a friend or follow them back.

- **Recent Players**—Lists people you've recently interacted with while playing online games.

- **Find Someone**—Enables you to search for a gamertag and more easily locate specific players in your friends list. Once you start entering characters, people you're friends with whose gamertag matches the characters you're entering start appearing, so you rarely have to type out a whole gamertag when locating friends.

- **My Profile**—Pulls up your profile. For more about your profile, turn to the "Understanding Your Profile" section in Chapter 4, "Personalizing Your Xbox One Experience."

- **Messages**—Provides easy access to the messages you've received.

Interacting with Friends

You can have up to 1,000 friends on your Xbox One, which is far more than you could have on the Xbox 360. Adding friends is a great way to personalize your Xbox experience and make the most of your console's connectivity and social features. If you already have an Xbox Live account, your friends automatically follow you onto your Xbox One console when you sign in to your account, and you can immediately start interacting with them.

Add a Friend

To add friends, follow these steps:

1. Make sure you are signed in to the profile you want to add friends to. Then select the Social tile from the Home screen.

2. Select Find Someone.

3. Use the onscreen keyboard to enter the gamertag of the person you want to add and then select Search.

4. Assuming your search finds a match, select Add Friend. (If it doesn't find a match, make sure you've entered the gamertag correctly or try another gamertag.)

5. Select Don't Show This Message Again if you don't want to see this notice every time you add a new friend, and then select Close. Otherwise, just select Close.

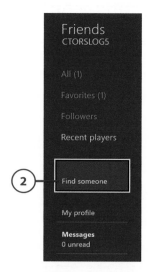

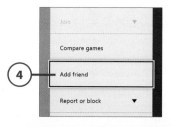

Ways of Interacting with Friends

Once you've added a friend and are in his or her profile, several options are available to you if you want to interact with your friend or make modifications:

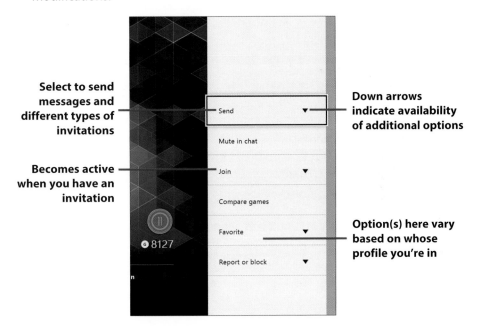

Select to send messages and different types of invitations

Send

Down arrows indicate availability of additional options

Mute in chat

Becomes active when you have an invitation

Join

Compare games

© 8127

Favorite

Option(s) here vary based on whose profile you're in

Report or block

- **Send**—Selecting Send provides you with several options for interacting with your friend. You can send your friend a message on his or her Xbox (see the "Send a Message" section later in this chapter). You can also send him or her a Party & Game Invite, a Party Invite, or a Game Invite. For more on sending these invitations, turn to the "Getting the Party Started" section later in this chapter.

- **Mute in Chat**—Selecting this option does exactly what it describes— mutes a person in chat so that you can no longer hear him or her. Keep in mind, if there is someone you want to hear in chat but can't, make sure this option isn't selected for him or her. More importantly, don't smack talk the person(s) you've muted because they can still hear you unless they've decided to mute you as well.

- **Join**—This option is grayed out unless the person sent you a Party & Game Invite, a Party Invite, or a Game Invite, and only the type of invitation sent is actually accessible from the menu of invitation options.

- **Compare Games**—This option enables you to see how you stack up against your friend with regard to the games you've both played.

- **Favorite, Friend, Add Friend**—What you see here depends on whose profile you're viewing. If the person is already a Favorite, you have two options: Remove from Favorites and Remove Friend. If the person is a Friend, your options are Add to Favorites and Remove Friend. If you're viewing the profile of a recent player (a stranger you recently gamed with online), you have the option to Add Friend.

- **Report or Block**—Selecting this option enables you to block or report someone. Blocking someone prevents the individual from making contact or otherwise interacting with you. When you report someone, you're filing a complaint with Xbox Live because you feel the person has violated the Xbox Live Code of Conduct (www.xbox.com/en-US/legal/codeofconduct). There are specific options for reporting an offensive player name or gamertag, player picture, or voice communication; cheating; unsportsmanlike behavior; and quitting early. The Xbox Live team reviews complaints and takes action if deemed necessary; however, it's probably wise to discuss any grievances directly with an individual before filing a complaint, particularly if they're a friend.

Adding Favorites

If you have difficulty locating your closest buddies, be sure to add them to your Favorites so that they always appear at the top of any friends listing. You can also easily find the friends you're looking for by selecting Find Someone and inputting their gamertag.

Send a Message

Once you have friends, followers, or recent players logged on your console, you can start interacting with them. To send these individuals a text message, follow these steps:

1. Sign in to your Xbox Live account.

2. From the Home screen, select the Social tile.

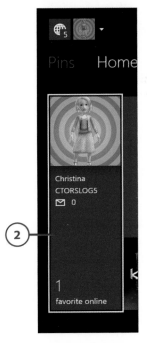

3. Locate the individual you want to send a message to and press the A button on your controller; scroll down if you need to. If you have a lot of people on your Friends list, it may be easier to use the Find Someone option and then enter the individual's gamertag.

4. Select the Send option.

5. From the drop-down menu, select Message.

6. Use the onscreen keyboard to enter your message and select Enter.

7. Select Send.

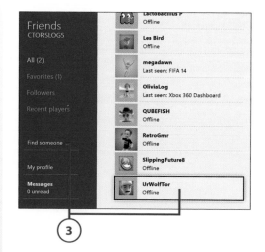

Making Message Sending Easier

You can also send your friend a message by selecting that person's gamertag from your Friends list, pressing the Menu button on your controller, and then selecting Send Message. If you have a USB keyboard (see the "Accessorizing Your Xbox One" section in Chapter 4) or Smart-Glass set up with a smartphone, you can more quickly and easily enter the message than with your controller. Turn to Chapter 11, "Looking Through the SmartGlass," for more on SmartGlass.

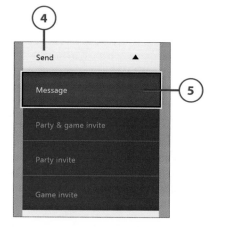

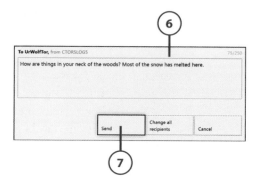

Learning About Your Friends

It can be easier to converse with your friends when you have a better idea of what they're into. The Friends app makes this task easy, as it enables you to learn more about your friends' activities. Here's what you can see when in a friend's profile (or anyone else's for that matter) when you scroll to the right, provided he or she has been active on the console (if not, some of these may not be available):

Recent Activity   **Game Clips**   **Friends**

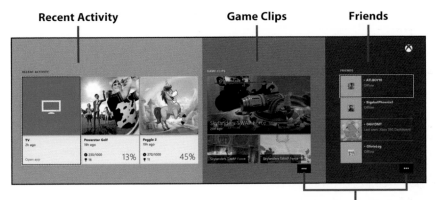

**Select these icons to see the
full list of available items for
each category**

- **Recent Activity**—This area shows you which activities your friend has recently engaged in. Select an activity to learn more details, such as how long your friend has engaged in the activity, his or her progress, and the achievements received. If your friend has not engaged in any activities, you won't see this information. Also, there are some activities for which you won't be able to get more details.

- **Game Clips**—Here, you can watch game clips of games that your friend has played. Once you finish watching a clip, the following options are provided: Replay, if you want to watch the clip again; Play This Game, if you want to obtain the game; Show Profile, if you want to see your friend's profile; More Clips from This Creator, if you want to see more of your friend's game clips; and Upload Home, if you want to go to your Upload Studio.

- **Friends**—See the people your friend is connected with. If you see someone you want to connect with, select that individual to access his or her profile, and then select Add Friend.

Getting the Party Started

Parties enable you to chat with your friends through your Xbox One console and play online games together. You can do this with just one friend or with up to seven friends; so up to eight microphones can be active at any given time. In addition, to start or join a party, you and your friends must have an active Xbox Live Gold membership and be signed in with the gamertag associated with that membership.

You can send your friends three different types of party invitations: a Party Invite, which invites them to chat with you; a Game Invite, which invites them to play a game with you; and a Party & Game Invite, which invites them to both chat and game. When a friend accepts your party invitation, his or her chat is turned on by default, so he or she can immediately start chatting with you. And if you've invited your friend to a game, he or she is taken right to the multiplayer setup for that game, enabling you and your friends to start gaming together.

Send a Party Invitation

You can only send party invitations to people who are currently online. To send a party invitation, follow these steps:

1. From the Home screen, select the Social tile.

2. Select the friend you want to invite to your party. You'll be able to invite others to the party once the invitation is sent.

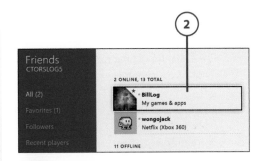

3. Select Send, and then select Party Invite. (If available and desired, you can instead opt to send a Party & Game Invite or a Game Invite; for more on this, see the "Invite a Friend to a Game" sections later in this chapter.)

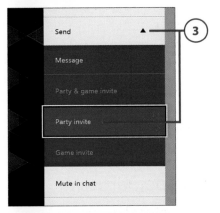

4. Your party invitation has been sent and is awaiting the invitee to join. In the meantime, if you want to invite additional people, select Invite to Party and proceed to step 5.

5. Select the other friends you want to invite and then select Party. Those people are now invited as well.

Chatting Through Kinect Versus a Headset

When you have a headset connected, you can't chat through Kinect, as the console assumes that you want that audio to be private and automatically turns off Kinect chat audio.

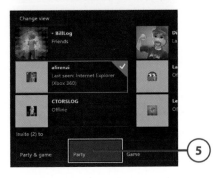

>>>Go Further

NUMEROUS WAYS TO START THE PARTY

As is typical with the Xbox, there are many ways to accomplish the same task. If you prefer, you can also start a party by going into your Friends list, selecting the profile of the friend you want to game with, and then selecting Invite to Party. Or you can select a friend from your Friends feed and then select Invite to Party.

If you want to invite multiple friends at once, you can accomplish this task more easily by selecting the Snap tile from the Home screen, selecting Party, and then selecting Invite to Party. This pulls up your list of friends, as shown in step 5 of "Send a Party Invitation." You can then simply select the friends you want to invite and then send them the desired type of invitation. And, finally, if you prefer to use your voice to launch a party, you can simply say, "Go to Party."

Joining Parties

Once you have a pool of friends, you'll undoubtedly be invited to Xbox Live parties. You can accept these invitations in numerous ways:

- **Look for party invitation pop-ups**—When you see a party invitation notification appear at the bottom of your screen, briefly hold the Xbox button to accept the invitation.

When you see this message, you have a party invite

- **Check your notifications**—The Notification mini-tile appears at the very top of the screen to the left of the Gamertag mini-tile. When you select it, you'll see if you have any party invitations. If so, you can opt to join any active parties by selecting that party so that Launch is shown and then pressing the A button on your controller. Keep in mind that expired parties may still be listed.

Scroll to the party you want so that it says Launch and then press the A button to select the party

Indicates an expired party

- **Check your friend's profile**—When you're in a friend's profile, you can see whether he or she is in a party. If so and you'd like to join it, you can do so by selecting the In a Party tile.

This Xbox Live friend is already in a party

Invite Friends to a Game from the Home Screen

If you want to game with your friends, you can send them a game invitation. Of course, only players who actually have the game can participate in the game. There are two ways to do this, one of those is from the Home screen, as in the following steps:

A More Specific Example

To see exactly how this process works, using the game *Killer Instinct* as an example, see the next section.

1. Select and launch an online multi-player game to play with your friends, keeping in mind that only friends who own the game can participate in the game.

2. Press the Xbox button to go to the Home screen and select the Party tile. If it doesn't appear on the Home screen, go to the My Games & Apps tile and select it from there.

3. Select Invite to Party.

4. Select the people you want to invite to the party and then select Game. When you go back to the game lobby, your friends should now be able to join in the game.

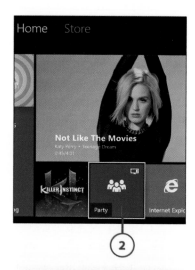

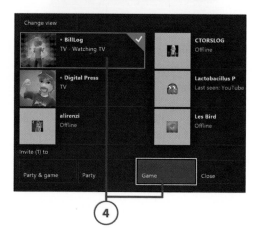

It's Not All Good

Challenges with Game Invites

Although you can sometimes send your friends a Game Invite directly from the Social area, such as if you're in a friend's profile (see "Send a Party Invitation" earlier in this chapter), this isn't always reliable. You might, at times, find this option grayed out, and at other times it might not work. Therefore, the best option is to send the invitation directly from the game itself (see the next section), though this can pose its own set of challenges, depending on the game's design.

Likewise, the Invite Party to Game option might not always be accessible either. This is because different games have different game lobbies, or areas where you must go to invite your friend or party to play a game. In addition, in some cases, you might have to create a mission or event before you can proceed with the invitation. If you run into difficulty, consult your game manual or try to send the invitation from different areas of the game.

Wondering why this is all so difficult? This is because in-game lobbies are completely separate from Xbox Live Party. They operate on different servers, so your invitees need to receive separate, specific invites that put them in the exact right place in a particular piece of software or application.

Invite Friends to a Game from in the Game

Now let's look at how to send a game invite from within a game. This process varies from game to game, so this example is based on sending an invite using *Killer Instinct*. Follow these steps:

1. From the main game menu, select Online Multiplayer.

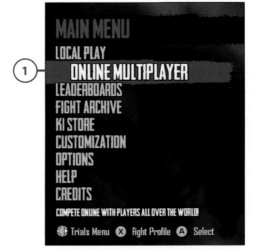

2. Select Exhibition Match.

3. Select Host/Invite. The game now creates a lobby for you.

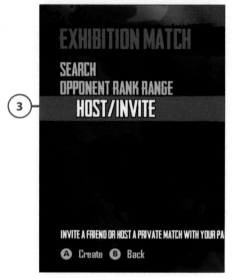

4. Select the people you want to invite and then select Game.

5. Your game invitation has now been sent. Once your party arrives, the games can begin.

Want to Know More About *Killer Instinct*?

Killer Instinct is a button-mashing fighting game that you can download for free. To learn more about the game, see its description in "Perusing Digital-Only Games" in Chapter 5, "Getting Your Game On."

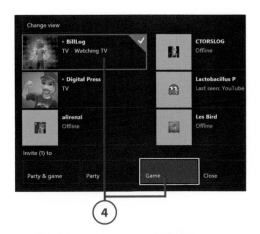

Keeping in Touch via Skype

Skype is what is commonly referred to by technophiles as a VoIP (Voice over Internet Protocol) service. As such, you can use Skype to communicate with friends, family, and other persons via voice chat, video messaging, and instant messaging over the Internet. If the individual you're communicating with is on Skype, which is available on a slew of platforms, voice and video chatting are free. If the person doesn't have a Skype account, you can still call his or her mobile or landline; however, this has costs, though they're likely considerably less expensive than using a landline. For more information on the available Skype plans, features, and costs, visit www.skype.com/intl/en-us/prices/.

And here's what's really cool about Skyping on your Xbox One: Because Skype is now owned by Microsoft, your Xbox One is optimized to make the best use of this service. Not only does a Skype tile come preinstalled on your console, but your Kinect's capabilities make for an ideal Skype-on-TV experience.

Set Up Skype

Although a Skype tile comes pre-installed on your console, you still need to install and set up your Skype account. To do so, follow these steps:

1. Go to the Pins area of the Home screen and select the Skype tile; unless you unpinned Skype, this is where you'll find it.

2. At the Skype App Details screen, select Install.

3. Once Skype is installed, select Launch.

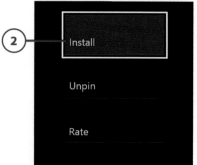

4. If you already have a Skype account, select Sign In. If you don't already have a Skype account, select Join.

5. Enter all the required information using the onscreen keyboard. If using a previous Skype account, go to step 6. Otherwise, proceed to step 7.

6. Select Link Accounts to link your Skype account with your Microsoft account.

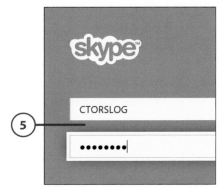

7. Select OK.

8. Decide whether you want to receive Skype notifications. We recommend that you allow them to ensure you never miss a call or message. You're now in Skype!

Look for Microsoft Skype Specials

During the launch window of the Xbox One, Microsoft gave Xbox Live Gold subscribers an added bonus of Skype Premium for free for 6 months, enabling group video calls and 100 minutes of telephone calling to some 60 countries. Although this offer expired in March of 2014, be sure to keep your eyes open for similar offers. With Microsoft owning Skype, it is likely that other bonus offers will be made available to new console owners in the future.

Examining the Skype Interface

After you successfully log in to your Skype account, you see the application screen, which contains the following elements:

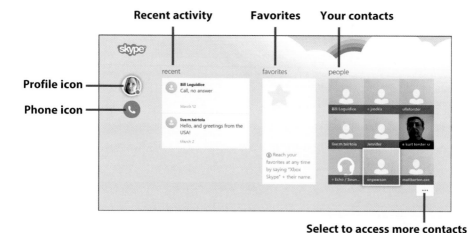

Recent activity   **Favorites**   **Your contacts**

Profile icon

Phone icon

Select to access more contacts

- **Profile icon**—Select this icon to access your profile. From the profile screen, you can edit your profile message, which is the message people who view your profile see; change your Skype status, whether you want to be available or invisible (if you don't want anyone Skyping you); add money to your Skype account; and adjust your privacy settings.

- **Phone icon**—Select this icon to make a call. It pulls up a menu to enter a phone number and to access your contacts.

- **Recent**—See recent activity/messages you've received, including invitations to connect. Skype now saves up to 1,000 messages, ensuring you don't miss an opportunity to connect with your friends and family.

- **Favorites**—Any people you've listed as Favorites on your Friends list and who have Skype appear here.

- **People**—Here, you'll find your Skype contacts. When you go to the full listing by selecting the More icon, you can see who is available to chat by selecting the Available option at the top of the screen.

Make a Voice and Video Call

Making Skype voice and video calls via your Xbox One is as easy as pie. Just follow these steps:

1. Sign in to the Xbox Live account you want to use to make the call and then select the Skype tile.

2. Select the Phone icon on the left side of the screen.

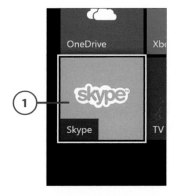

3. Enter the phone number of the person you want to call or select View Contacts and then select the person you want to call.

4. Select Voice Call or Video Call, depending on which type of call you'd like to make.

5. Skype will now try to connect your voice or video call.

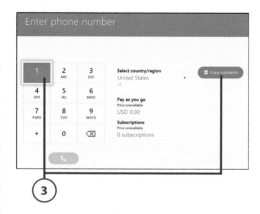

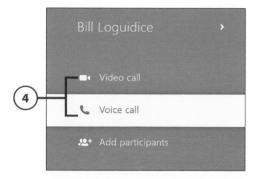

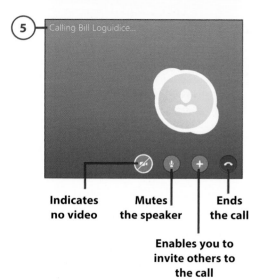

Indicates no video

Mutes the speaker

Ends the call

Enables you to invite others to the call

Accepting Skype Calls

You can accept Skype calls using a controller or via voice command:

- **Using your controller**—When a call notification appears onscreen, press and hold the Xbox button on the controller to view the incoming call details. A window then pops up from which you can select Answer or Answer Without Video, depending on your preference. If you don't want to accept the call, select Close.

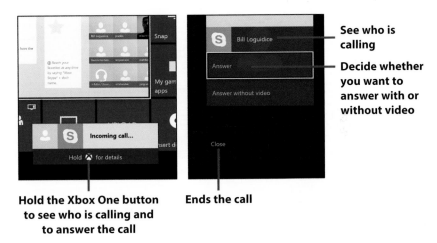

See who is calling

Decide whether you want to answer with or without video

Hold the Xbox One button to see who is calling and to answer the call

Ends the call

- **Using your voice**—When a call notification appears onscreen, say either "Xbox, answer" or "Xbox, answer without video."

Send a Text Message

If you don't feel like chatting but want to communicate with a contact, you can easily send him or her a text message. To send a text message, follow these steps:

1. From the Skype interface, go to People and select the contact you want to correspond with. If you have many contacts and don't see the contact you want, select the More icon to access your full list.

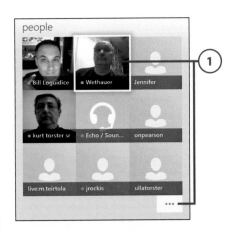

2. Scroll to and select the Emoticon icon. (Once you start typing, you can't add an emoticon. If you don't want to add one, select the Type a Message Here field and skip to step 5.)

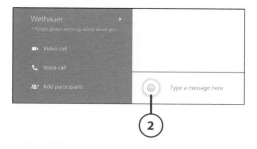

3. Select the emoticon(s) you'd like to include from the menu and then press B.

4. Select the message area and enter a message using the onscreen keyboard.

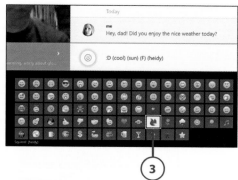

Easier Typing

If you have access to SmartGlass (see Chapter 11) you can use it to more easily enter your message.

5. Select Enter on the keyboard when you're ready to send the message.

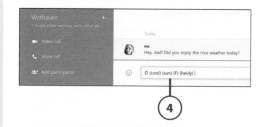

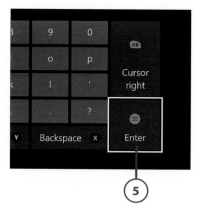

6. Your message now appears. Press B to go back to the main interface or continue to type additional messages.

**Navigate live TV
with OneGuide**

**Access various video
services to watch TV shows,
movies, web clips, and
sporting events**

**Rent or purchase
popular movies
and TV shows**

In this chapter, you learn about the Xbox One's video offerings, including movies, TV shows, web clips, and sports, as well as accessing your own media.

→ Working with OneGuide

→ Enjoying TV Shows, Music Videos, and Movies with Xbox Video

→ Using Apps to Watch Video

→ Playing DVDs and Blu-rays

Viewing Videos and Video Content

Your Xbox One is one of the best platforms to enjoy many different types of video, including movies, TV shows, web clips, and sporting events. Besides passing through and controlling video from your cable or satellite provider, you can also enjoy almost instant HD-quality video streams from a variety of apps. In addition, you can purchase, download, and watch selections from a large content library, as well as play your own DVDs or Blu-rays.

Working with OneGuide

OneGuide allows you to watch live television from your cable or satellite box while simultaneously taking advantage of the extended apps and features of your Xbox One. See "Setting Up a Cable or Satellite Connection" in Chapter 1, "Setting Up Your Xbox One," and "TV & OneGuide" under "Changing the Console Settings" in Chapter 2, "Navigating Your Xbox One's Dashboard and Settings," for first-time setup. Refer to "Understanding Kinect Controls" in Chapter 2 for the basics of how to navigate OneGuide with motion and voice commands. OneGuide can be displayed by either saying, "Xbox, OneGuide," or, when watching TV full screen, by pressing the Menu button on the controller and selecting OneGuide.

See only the channels or apps set as Favorites

See all TV listings

See what's on the video apps you've installed and run

When OneGuide controls content from your cable or satellite box, it doesn't enforce content restrictions for playback you've associated with your Xbox One profile. If you want to configure parental controls for what you watch on your TV, you should do so directly on your cable or satellite box. Contact your cable or satellite provider if you have any questions about this process. What OneGuide does filter are explicit titles and descriptions in its listings. This setting is on by default for all accounts. To view or change this setting, go to Settings, then select Privacy and Online Safety. Refer to "Breaking Down the Settings Screen" in Chapter 2 for more information.

Add and Watch Your Favorite Channels

The TV listings that OneGuide displays show you all of the channels available to you based on your selected TV provider and channel lineup. The Favorites option allows you to set a list of favorite channels for quick access. To add your favorite channels, start OneGuide and then follow these steps:

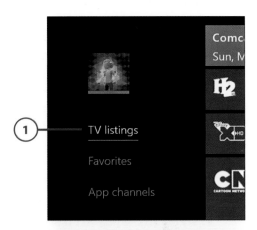

1. Select TV Listings from the options to the left of the main OneGuide screen.

2. Scroll through the available channels column to select the channel, or say, "Xbox," and then the name of the channel.

3. Once the desired channel is selected, say, "Xbox, add to favorites," or press the A button on the controller.

Removing a Favorite

To remove a Favorite, repeat these steps, but instead of selecting or saying Add to Favorites in step 3, select or say Remove from Favorites.

Watching Your Favorites

To watch your Favorites after starting OneGuide, say, "Xbox, favorites," or select Favorites from the options to the left of the main OneGuide screen.

FILTERING SD OR HD CHANNELS

Even though your Xbox One, by default, requires an HD television with a resolution of 720p or better, your cable or satellite box has no such requirements. This means that even though you have an HDTV, you'll still be offered lower-quality, SD broadcasts on your cable or satellite box along with the preferred HD ones. Although some cable or satellite boxes have modes to automatically jump to an HD version of an SD channel if one is available, you can filter your channels based on definition directly through OneGuide. Refer to "TV & OneGuide" in Chapter 2 for more information on changing how the channels are filtered.

Using App Channels to See Your Streaming Video Apps

Besides live TV, OneGuide also integrates the programming from your favorite streaming video apps into your channel lineup. Apps like Xbox Video, Netflix, and Hulu Plus have listings just like a regular TV channel with available videos that appear to the right of the channel listing. After you download, install, and run one of these video apps for the first time, it is automatically added to the OneGuide App Channels list.

Scroll up and down this column to see available App Channels

The selected App Channel's programming appears to the right

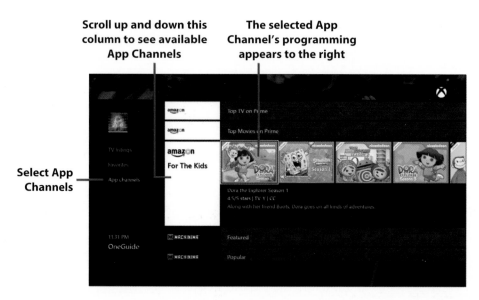

Select App Channels

To find App Channels, start OneGuide, then say, "Xbox, app channels," or select App Channels from the options to the left of the main OneGuide screen.

Enjoying TV Shows, Music Videos, and Movies with Xbox Video

Using the Xbox Video app, you can buy or rent TV shows and movies right on your Xbox One console. Xbox Video content is also available via apps on Xbox 360, Windows 8 PCs and tablets, as well as Windows Phone 8 devices. Finally, using a Windows 7 or later, or Mac OS X v10.6.8 or later, computer, Xbox Video content can also be accessed via the XboxVideo.com website. Some of the nicer features of Xbox Video include the ability to quickly search over 150,000 titles with Bing, TV Season Passes that can offer a savings of up to 20% to 50% off the individual episode prices, closed captioning for most TV shows and movies, and, for select titles, SmartGlass-enhanced interactive content and other extras.

Purchase or Rent Media

Buying or renting TV shows or movies works in a manner similar to purchasing other content on your Xbox One. To rent or buy content using the Xbox Video app, follow these steps:

1. From the Home screen, scroll right to select the Movies & TV tile.

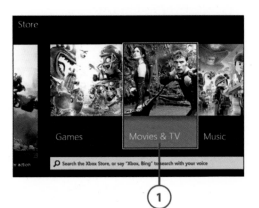

1

2. Select Xbox Video.

3. From the Xbox Video Home screen, do a Video Search, or browse and select a title from the Recommendations, Featured Sets, Collection, Movies Store, or TV Store categories. Once you select a title, all of its details are available, including applicable ratings, descriptions, cast lists, and trailers.

4. Select the Buy (or Rent) option for the title. Much like with games, you can also provide your own rating, from one (worst) to five (best) stars. You can decide whether to purchase or rent the media in HD or SD, the former of which is the default setting. You can, in some cases, even watch a trailer for the video.

5. Follow the remaining prompts to complete your purchase or rental transaction, which is charged immediately, with no ability to procure a refund.

Limitations

If renting, the viewing period is 14 days from the time of your order or 48 hours from the time you start to watch, whichever happens first, and is only available on the system it was rented on. Purchased content can be used on a maximum of up to five compatible devices.

Controlling Playback

While Kinect (see "Understanding Kinect Controls" in Chapter 2), a media remote (see "Accessorizing Your Xbox One" in Chapter 4, "Personalizing Your Xbox One Experience"), or SmartGlass (see Chapter 11, "Looking Through the SmartGlass") provides the most intuitive control options, you can also use the wireless controller. Once your video starts, the following controller functions are available:

Video information

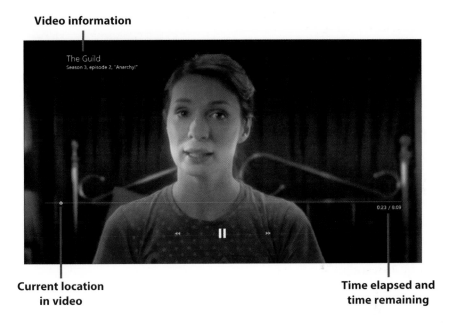

Current location in video

Time elapsed and time remaining

- **Left stick, View button, X button, Y button, A button, D-pad, or right stick**—Shows the playback overlay.

- **A button**—When the playback overlay is displayed, pauses or resumes video playback.

- **Left stick or D-pad**—When the playback overlay is displayed, moves left and right between the Rewind, Pause/Play, and Fast Forward options. Press the A button to activate the highlighted option.

- **Left trigger**—Rewinds. Press again for faster rewinding, up to the maximum speed. Press the A button to resume normal playback. When the video is paused and the left trigger is pressed, it rewinds at the slowest speed.

- **Right trigger**—Fast-forwards. Press again for faster fast-forwarding, up to the maximum speed. Press the A button to resume normal playback. When the video is paused and the right trigger is pressed, it fast-forwards at the slowest speed.

- **B button**—Goes back to the video's Home screen.

- **Menu button**—Displays the Xbox Video app options.

When you press the Menu button, the following options are available:

The Xbox Video app options

- **Video Home**—Goes back to the video's Home screen

- **Restore My Purchases**—Restores access to your previously purchased content

- **Help**—Displays Xbox Video app help

- **About**—Displays the Xbox Video app's copyright notice and related information

- **Feedback**—Provides feedback on whether you like or dislike the Xbox Video app and your optional suggestions for improving it

>>>Go Further

CLOSED CAPTIONS

Closed captions let you read the words that are spoken in the audio portion of a video and often include other descriptors that identify speakers and background noises. When closed captioning is turned on, captions are usually displayed at the bottom of your display. If you enable closed captions on your Xbox One, you'll see the captions on all closed caption-enabled video content that you play on your console. To turn on closed captions, go to Settings and select Closed Captioning. Closed captions can be further personalized by selecting Use Custom Style and following the onscreen instructions.

Stream Videos and Photos from Your Computer

Your Xbox One can stream videos or photos from a Windows 7 or later computer to Xbox Video. To do so, open the Settings app and follow these steps:

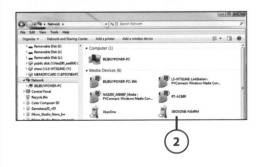

1. Under Preferences, ensure that Allow Play to Streaming is checked.

2. Open a File Explorer window on your computer. Make sure your Xbox One is visible as a media device on the same network that your computer is on. The name listed will be the name given to your Xbox One in the System section of the Settings app; the default name is XboxOne.

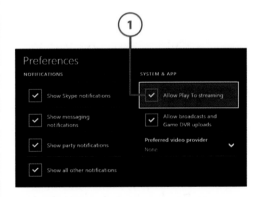

Console Not Visible

If your console isn't visible, ensure that both your computer and your Xbox One are connected to the same network and try again.

3. Locate the video or picture file on your computer or other accessible network location and right-click it. From the menu that appears, select Play To and then the name of your Xbox One. Xbox Video will start automatically on your console.

Supported File Formats

Most common video formats, such as AVI, MKV, MP4, MPG, and WMV, should stream without issue, as well as most picture formats, such as JPG, PNG, and BMP. Multiple files can also be selected to queue.

4. The Play To dialog box is shown on your computer as the video or picture files play on your Xbox One. Use the Xbox Video app's controls to control the video or picture on your Xbox One's display.

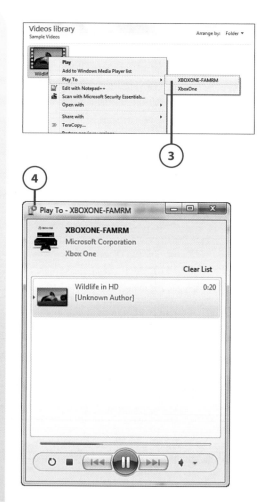

It's Not All Good

What About Other Streaming Options?

On the market since November 22, 2005, the Xbox 360 has evolved over time to support an impressive range of media streaming options. Unfortunately, as with several of the other current features on the relatively new Xbox One, it's noticeably lacking in many of the same media streaming options that made its predecessor so great. On the plus side, Microsoft has promised, at minimum, feature parity in the future with the Xbox 360 for media streaming as new features continue to be added.

Stream Videos from a Mobile Device

You can also stream video from most Android or iOS mobile devices using a free app called Skitfa. To stream videos or photos from the Skitfa app for Android or iOS mobile devices, do the following:

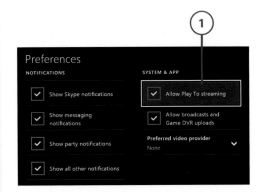

1. On the Xbox One, go to Settings, Preferences, and ensure that Allow Play To Streaming is checked.

Installing the App

These steps assume that you've already downloaded and installed the Skitfa app to your mobile device.

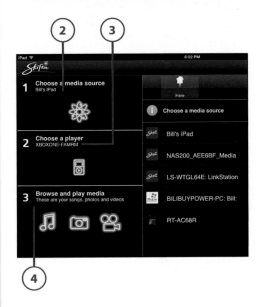

2. In the Skifta app, under Choose a Media Source, select your media source from the available choices. These options include the mobile device its running on or any available computers or network locations. (The look of your device's Skifta app may differ slightly from the example.)

3. Select the name of your Xbox One under Choose a Player.

4. Select the media file under Browse and Play Media. Your Xbox One will now play the selection. Xbox Video will start automatically on your console.

What About Music Files?

The steps for streaming common audio files, like MP3 or WMA, from your Windows computer or a mobile device using Skifta works exactly the same as they do for video or picture files. Instead of running the Xbox Video app, run the Xbox Music app (see Chapter 8, "Tuning In to Music"), then choose an audio file instead of a video or picture file.

Using Apps to Watch Video

Your Xbox One features an ever-growing selection of the top video streaming services available today, several of which are described in the sections that follow. Just as with Xbox Video, a media remote, Kinect, or SmartGlass provide the most intuitive controls for these various services. Nevertheless, as before, the instructions you find here focus on using the controller as we know you've got it and it consistently works as advertised.

Netflix

You know Netflix. It's the most popular video rental service running. It provides DVDs and Blu-rays by mail, and offers a streaming option for computers, mobile devices, and set-top boxes such as the Xbox One. There are two requirements for Netflix streaming on your Xbox One. The first is that you're an Xbox Live Gold member. The second is that you have an unlimited streaming Netflix account, which, if you don't already have one, you can sign up by following the instructions that follow.

Download and Activate the Netflix App

To download and activate Netflix, locate it in the Store and follow these steps:

1. Install Netflix from its App Details screen.

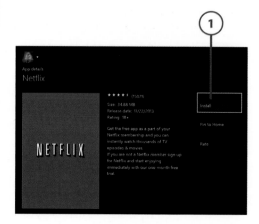

2. Start the Netflix app and select Member Sign In. Enter your Netflix email address and password, then select Sign In.

Signing Up

If you are not already a Netflix member, select Start Your Free Month instead of Member Sign In. Use your web browser to visit http://netflix.com/xboxone and follow the instructions. Once you have entered the information to start your free trial from the website, select Sign In on your Xbox One and follow the remaining instructions.

Navigating Netflix

Once you have logged in to Netflix and started the app, you need to select a profile if more than one is on the account. Profiles are a way for Netflix to keep watch histories and recommendations separate for multiple family members who use the same Netflix account. Once you select a profile, you are presented with the main Netflix screen.

Scroll left to show My List and other categories

Current selection

Scroll right for more categories

Search

Netflix is broken up into categories, which you can access by scrolling right. Conduct searches by selecting Search or press the Y button on the gamepad. Select Change Profile or press the X button to switch profiles. Select Browse Kids to limit selections to only family friendly content. Pressing the Menu button on the controller displays the Netflix app options, which include Search Netflix, Change Netflix Profile, Settings, Help, and Exit Netflix.

Once a video is selected, its Home screen is displayed. From this screen, you can select Play, or, if it has more than one entry, which episode you'd like to play. Selecting Add to My List adds it to the My List category, which is a list of items you set for quick access for later viewing. Rate lets you add your own rating for the selected program, which replaces the average user rating in red.

As with Xbox Video, a full complement of Kinect, media remote, and Smart-Glass functionality are available, but you can also use the wireless controller. Once your video starts, the following controller functions are active:

- **Left stick, X button, Y button, A button, D-pad, or right stick**—Shows the playback overlay.

- **A button**—When the playback overlay is displayed, pauses or resumes video playback.

- **Left stick or D-pad**—When the playback overlay is displayed, moves left and right between the Rewind, Pause/Play, Fast Forward, and Closed Captioning (if available) options. Press the A button to activate the highlighted option.

- **Left trigger**—Rewinds. Press again for faster rewinding, up to the maximum speed. Press the A button to resume normal playback. When the video is paused and the left trigger is pressed, it rewinds at the slowest speed.

- **Right trigger**—Fast-forwards. Press again for faster fast-forwarding, up to the maximum speed. Press the A button to resume normal playback. When the video is paused and the right trigger is pressed, it fast-forwards at the slowest speed.

- **B button**—Goes back to the video's Home screen.

- **Menu button**—Displays the Netflix app options.

Hulu Plus

Hulu Plus is a subscription service that offers ad-supported, on-demand streaming of TV shows, movies, and other videos, including trailers and web shows. Hulu Plus has two requirements for your Xbox One. The first is that you must be an Xbox Live Gold member. The second is that you must have a Hulu Plus account, which, if you don't already have one, you can sign up on your console.

It's Not All Good

Why Don't Some Videos Play?

Hulu Plus doesn't have the rights to stream every video to devices other than computer web browsers. If you encounter such a video, it will be flagged as "Web-Only" content and will only be viewable on a computer.

Download and Activate the Hulu Plus App

To download and activate Hulu Plus, locate Hulu Plus in the Store and follow these steps:

1. Select Install from the Hulu Plus App Details screen.

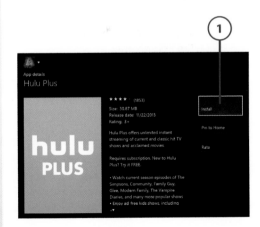

2. Select Launch from this same screen, once the app is installed.

3. If you are already a Hulu Plus member, choose Log In and enter the onscreen code at www.hulu.com/activate, or select Log In with your email address and password and follow the instructions.

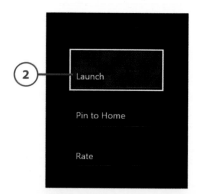

Becoming a Member

If you're not already a Hulu Plus member, select Try 1 Week Free and enter the onscreen code at www.hulu.com/activate, or select Sign Up on This Device and follow the remaining instructions. You'll need a credit card or PayPal account to start the one-week trial, which you can cancel after the trial period is over if you don't want to pay for the service.

Select to see a quick tour of the service

Navigating Hulu Plus

Once you have logged in to Hulu Plus and started the app, you're presented with the main Hulu Plus screen.

Search

Scroll down or right for more categories

Hulu Plus is organized by categories, which you can access by scrolling down or right. Conduct searches by selecting the Search box. Pressing the Menu button on the controller displays the Hulu Plus app options, which include Search, Settings, and Help.

Once a video is selected, it starts playing. As with the other video services, Kinect, media remote, and SmartGlass functionality are all available, as well as the wireless controller. Once a video starts, the following controller functions are active:

- **A button**—Shows the playback overlay. When the playback overlay is displayed, pauses or resumes video playback.

- **Left stick or D-pad**—When the playback overlay is displayed, moves left and right between the Rewind, Pause/Play, Fast Forward, and Closed Captioning (if available) options. Press the A button to activate the highlighted option.

- **Left trigger**—Rewinds. Press again for faster rewinding, up to the maximum speed. Press the A button to resume normal playback. When the video is paused and the left trigger is pressed, it rewinds at the slowest speed.

- **Right trigger**—Fast-forwards. Press again for faster fast-forwarding, up to the maximum speed. Press the A button to resume normal playback. When the video is paused and the right trigger is pressed, it fast-forwards at the slowest speed.

- **B button**—Goes to the video's Home screen, or main page. Beyond getting additional information about the program or series, you can also add the show to a queue or favorite it. Your queue holds all of the videos you plan on watching at a later time and is similar to a playlist. When you favorite something, when new episodes of a show are added to Hulu Plus, they will appear automatically in your queue.

- **Menu button**—Displays the Hulu Plus app options.

It's Not All Good

What About the Ads?

Unfortunately, watching the ads are mandatory on Hulu Plus. As a result, only Play, Pause, and Stop functions are available when an ad is running.

Amazon Instant Video

With an Amazon Prime Instant Video subscription, you not only gain access to a Netflix-like selection of streaming TV shows and movies, but also the ability to purchase content, get free 2-day shipping and reduced cost 1-day shipping on eligible Amazon.com purchases, and, for Kindle device owners, access to the Lending Library, which enables you to borrow select books.

On the Xbox One, as long as you're an Xbox Live Gold member, you'll have access to all available streaming content as long as you maintain a Prime subscription, and, with or without an active Prime subscription, access to any other digital video content you've purchased from Amazon Instant Video.

Download and Activate Amazon Instant Video

To download and activate Amazon Instant Video, locate the app in the Store and follow these steps:

1. Select Install from Amazon Instant Video's App Details screen.

2. Select the Launch button from this same screen, once the app is installed.

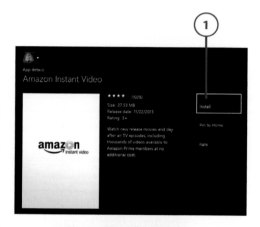

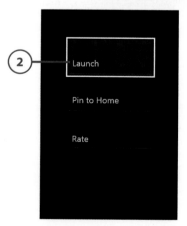

3. If you're already an Amazon Prime member, choose Sign In and Start Watching and follow the onscreen prompts.

Getting an Account

If you don't already have an Amazon account, go to www.amazon.com/watchonxboxone, then return to this sign in screen. If you'd rather browse the app's options, press the B button on your controller.

Navigating Amazon Instant Video

Once you have started Amazon Instant Video, you're presented with the app's main screen.

Amazon Instant Prime has three master categories: Prime Movies, Prime TV Shows, and Kid Zone. You can search by pressing the Y button on the controller or selecting Search after pressing the Menu button. The remaining sections are:

- **Your Watchlist**—These are programs you've added to your playlist for quick access or later viewing.

- **Recommendations**—These are Amazon's recommendations based on your viewing history.

- **Your TV Shows**—This is a listing of recently watched television shows.

- **Your Video Library**—This library displays any videos that you own.

- **Recently Watched**—This is a listing of all recently watched videos.

Pressing the Menu button on the controller displays the Amazon Instant Video app options, which include Home, Help, Switch User, and Sign Out.

Whether you purchase, rent, or have a video included as part of Amazon Instant Prime, once selected, its Home screen is displayed. From this screen, you can select Play, or, if it has more than one entry, which episode you'd like to play. As applicable, selecting Add to Watchlist or Add Season to Watchlist adds the single video or entire season of a show to the Your Watchlist category.

As with the other video services, Kinect, media remote, and SmartGlass functionality are all available, as well as the wireless controller. Once a video starts, the following controller functions are active:

- **A button**—Shows the playback overlay. When the playback overlay is displayed, pauses or resumes video playback.

- **Left stick or D-pad**—When the playback overlay is displayed, moves left and right between the Rewind, Pause/Play, Fast Forward, and Closed Captioning (if available) options. Press the A button to activate the highlighted option.

- **Left trigger**—Rewinds. Press again for faster rewinding, up to the maximum speed. Press the A button to resume normal playback. When the video is paused and the left trigger is pressed, it rewinds at the slowest speed.

- **Right trigger**—Fast-forwards. Press again for faster fast-forwarding, up to the maximum speed. Press the A button to resume normal playback. When the video is paused and the right trigger is pressed, it fast-forwards at the slowest speed.

- **X button or B button**—Quits playback and goes to the video's Home screen. Beyond getting additional information about the program or series, you can also add the show to a queue or favorite it. Your queue holds all of the videos you plan on watching at a later time and is similar to a playlist. When you favorite something, when new episodes of a show are added to Amazon Instant Video, they will appear automatically in your queue.

- **Menu button**—Displays the Amazon Instant Video app options.

YouTube

YouTube features a mass of original videos on nearly every subject imaginable uploaded by both amateurs and professionals. Although a YouTube account is not a requirement to start watching videos, you do need an Xbox Live Gold membership. A YouTube account also allows you to share your saved Game DVR clips (refer to "Working with Game DVR, Upload, and Upload Studio" in Chapter 5, "Getting Your Game On") from the My Uploads section of the app.

Download and Sign In to the YouTube App

To download and optionally sign in to the YouTube app, locate the app in the Store and follow these steps:

1. Select Install from the YouTube App Details screen.

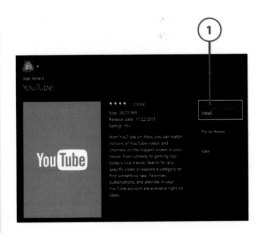

2. Select Launch from this same screen to start the YouTube app after it's installed.

3. You can sign in to the YouTube app with your Google account by selecting Sign In under the Sign In & Settings option and following the activation instructions. Once signed in, you'll have access to additional YouTube features, including your viewing history and any playlists or subscriptions.

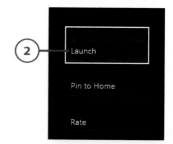

Navigating YouTube

Once you've started the YouTube app, you're presented with a screen of categories that you can scroll through by moving up or down, as well as any applicable personalization, like "My Watch Later Videos" if you're signed in. You can search by selecting the Search option or pressing the Y button on the controller.

Scroll up and down to move between categories and options

Scroll left and right to move between a category's content

As with the other video services, Kinect, media remote, and SmartGlass functionality are all available, as well as the wireless controller. Once you start playing a video, the following controller functions are active:

- **Menu button**—Pauses and resumes playback.

- **A button**—Shows the playback overlay. When the playback overlay is displayed, pauses or resumes video playback.

- **Left stick or D-pad**—When the playback overlay is displayed, moves left and right between the More actions (Subscribe, Like, Dislike, Flag as Inappropriate, Search), Go Home, Skip Backward, Rewind, Pause/Play, Forward, Skip Forward, and Closed Captioning (if available). Press the A button to activate the highlighted option.

- **Left trigger**—Rewinds. Press again for faster rewinding, up to the maximum speed. Press the A button to resume normal playback. When the video is paused and the left trigger is pressed, it rewinds at the slowest speed.

- **Right trigger**—Fast-forwards. Press again for faster fast-forwarding, up to the maximum speed. Press the A button to resume normal playback. When the video is paused and the right trigger is pressed, it fast-forwards at the slowest speed.

- **X button or B button**—Quits playback and goes to the app's Home screen.

- **Y button**—Searches for other videos.

Watching Other Video Services

As you can imagine, the services mentioned earlier in this chapter are just the tip of the video app iceberg. Microsoft continues to add new video apps to the Xbox One's lineup, each with their own sign in or subscription requirements. The best way to stay on top of any new video apps that you might be interested in is to regularly check the New Releases section of the Apps section of the Store.

Regularly check New Releases for additional video apps you might like

See more New Releases

The following are short descriptions of a representative sampling of the Xbox One's ever-growing list of video apps:

- **Bonnaroo**—Watch selections from the Bonnaroo live music festival.

- **Crackle**—Watch movies and TV on demand.

- **CW TV Now**—Check out your favorite CW network shows, including full episodes, previews, and interviews.

- **ESPN**—Access content from this service of the popular network. The app provides the latest news, scores, and stats centered around the teams and sports you care the most about.

- **FoxNow**—Check out your favorite Fox prime-time shows, including full episodes, previews, and interviews.

- **FXNow**—Access content from the FX, FXX, and FXM networks.

- **MLB.tv**—Watch every out-of-market regular season Major League Baseball game.

- **MUZU.TV**—Access to over 40,000 music videos, as well as music news and interviews.

- **NFL**—Check out official NFL news, video highlights and stories, live stats and scores, and even built-in NFL.com Fantasy Football functionality.

- **Redbox Instant by Verizon**—Browse, bookmark, and instantly stream movies, as well as find and reserve movies from Redbox locations near you.

- **TED**—More than 1,600 talks from famous movers and shakers in the education, technology, medical, business, music, and other fields.

- **Univision Deportes**—Access content from the popular Spanish-language American sports channel, which is centered around soccer and soccer-related programming.

- **VUDU Movies**—Rent new movies and TV shows.

Playing DVDs and Blu-rays

To watch DVDs or Blu-rays on your Xbox One for the first time, you must first install the Blu-ray Player app. You can install the app from the Apps category of the Store, or insert a DVD or Blu-ray disc, which automatically prompts you. Once the app is installed, you can watch DVD or Blu-ray discs by inserting the disc into your console and selecting the Blu-ray Player tile on the bottom-right corner of the Home screen.

Controlling DVDs and Blu-rays

Besides Kinect, media remote, and SmartGlass functionality, you can control DVD and Blu-ray playback with the wireless controller. The following controller functions are available when playing a DVD or Blu-ray:

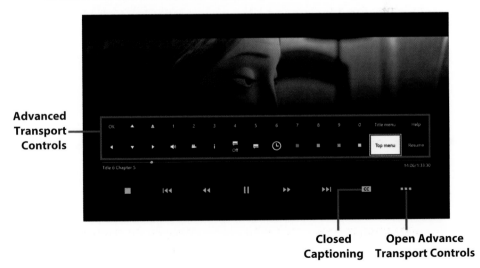

- **X button**—Pauses and resumes playback.

- **Left bumper**—Skips back one chapter. You can also press the B button, then select Skip Back.

- **Right bumper**—Skips forward one chapter. You can also press the B button, then select Skip Forward.

- **Right trigger**—Fast-forwards. Press the right trigger again to increase the speed.

- **Left trigger**—Rewinds. Press the left trigger again to increase the speed.

- **B button or Y button**—Opens the onscreen display playback controls. The Menu button also works for DVDs.

- **View button**—Opens the advanced transport controls, which include enabling subtitles, changing the camera angle, changing the audio channel, and displaying instant playback details. The options available vary by what is supported by the DVD.

The following commands are specific to Blu-rays:

- **Menu button**—Access the pop-up menu for discs that support this feature. Pressing right on the left stick or D-pad also works. Pressing left on the left stick or D-pad closes the pop-up menu.

- **Right on left stick, right on D-pad**—Access the track bar for discs that support this feature.

Create radio stations and playlists on Xbox Music

Listen to music and watch music videos

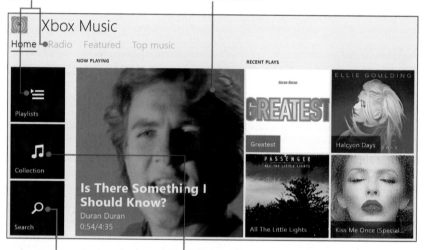

Find the music you want to listen to

Learn how to get your music collection on Xbox Music

In this chapter, you learn all about the Xbox Music app and how to use it to enhance your entertainment experience, as well how to play music CDs via the Audio CD Player app.

→ Accessing Xbox Music and Xbox Music Pass

→ Understanding the Xbox Music Interface

→ Playing Your Music CDs

Tuning In to Music

You might not immediately think of music when contemplating your Xbox One's capabilities, but your console enables you to enjoy music in multiple ways, from streaming songs from your PC or from Xbox Music's catalog of more than 30 million songs, to watching more than 92,000 music videos via Xbox Music, to simply inserting your favorite audio CD. In addition, with a Music Pass, you can also download music to your other devices, including those on Android- and iOS-based platforms, for offline use. In this chapter, you learn how to tap the full potential of your console's musical offerings.

Accessing Xbox Music and Xbox Music Pass

Xbox Music is Microsoft's cloud-based music service and, at the time of this writing, it's the only music service available on the Xbox One. So, there's not Spotify, LastFM, etc. Boo!

Fortunately, Xbox Music, which replaces Zune, Microsoft's previous music service, isn't half bad. Zune included a series of hardware devices and streaming services that were featured prominently on the Xbox 360.

Through Xbox Music, you can play free streaming radio, obtain paid music subscription services, and purchase music individually. But before you can fully partake in Xbox Music, you need an Xbox Live Gold membership and a Music Pass. Here's what this pass gives you:

- The ability to download as much music as you want from the Xbox Music Store and to listen to it without being interrupted by advertising.

- The ability to play your downloaded music on your computer and then sync it with up to four devices to play offline; these devices can use Windows, Android, or iOS operating systems.

- The ability to stream your own music from your PC. Yes, you actually need a Music Pass to do this. Some people have found workarounds, but they don't work smoothly.

- The ability to watch music videos on your Xbox One.

You can purchase a 1-month Music Pass for $9.99 or sign up for an annual membership for $99.90 (which is the most economical option if you plan on using the service a lot, averaging $8.33 per month). You can also buy gift cards at outside retailers like Amazon.com for other time intervals, such as a 3-month pass for $29.97.

Not Sure Whether to Invest in a Music Pass?

You can still explore what Xbox Music has to offer, even without a Music Pass. As long as you have an Xbox Live Gold membership, you can stream 15 tracks for free without the Music Pass. If you want to get a better sense of the service, you can also sign up for a 1-month free trial.

Install Xbox Music

Before you can access Xbox Music, you need to install it. Follow these steps:

1. Sign in to the account you want to use and then select the pre-pinned Xbox Music tile from the Pins section of the Home screen.

2. Select Install.

3. Select Launch.

4. Decide whether to Get Free Trial or to Explore. If you decide on the free trial, proceed to the next section in this chapter "Sign Up for an Xbox Music Pass."

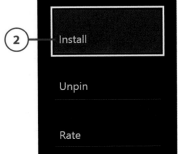

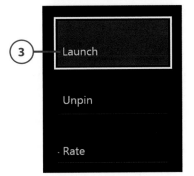

Sign Up for an Xbox Music Pass

If you want a 1-month free trial of the Music Pass, keep in mind that you have to enter your credit card information; Microsoft will automatically renew your subscription unless you cancel it before the end of the trial period. To get the trial, follow these steps:

1. Sign in to the account for which you want to obtain Xbox Music and then go to the Xbox Music app; if you haven't moved the app, it appears under the Pins section of the Home screen.

2. Select the Get Your Free Trial Today tile from the Xbox Music screen.

3. At the Subscription page, select Free Music Pass Trial. If you prefer to get a paid membership, choose between the 1-month and 12-month pass, or if you have an Xbox Music Pass gift card, you can select Use a Code.

4. Select Add a Credit Card.

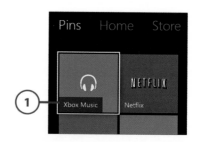

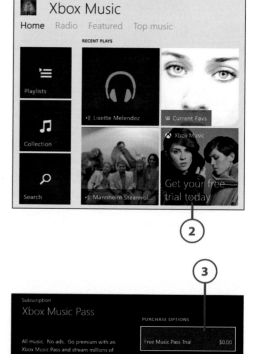

5. Use the onscreen keyboard to input the cardholder's name and then select Enter. Do the same with the screens that follow for your credit card number (enter without any spaces), expiration date, security code (appears on the back of the credit card), street address, city, state/province, postal code, phone number, and email address.

6. Confirm your billing information and select Save Info.

7. At the Buy Xbox Music Pass screen, select Confirm.

8. Select Get Free Trial or Get Started. You're now in Xbox Music.

Understanding the Xbox Music Interface

The Xbox Music app interface is clean and straightforward. The following options are available to you:

As you listen to music, it appears here, rather than the promotional material. If you're watching a video, it plays in this space as well.

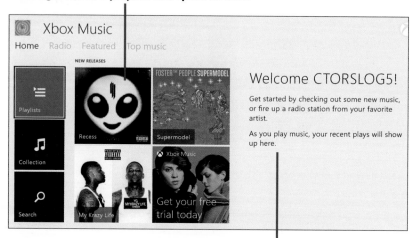

Audio and music video content you've recently played appears here for easy access.

- **Home**—This is the main screen from which you access all of Xbox Music's main features, which are described in the following bullet points.

- **Radio**—Select this option to create a radio station, which uses a favorite artist or group to create a station that includes music by that artist/group as well as similar artists. This is a good way to discover new music. If you don't care for a song that's playing, you can skip it. If fact, you can skip songs as many times as you want. For more on radio stations, see the "Create a Radio Station" section later in this chapter.

- **Featured**—Select this option to find new albums and new music videos. If you don't find what you're looking for, you can also conduct a search.

- **Top Music**—Select this option to access top music and top videos, which can be sorted by songs, albums, artists, and genre. If a song has an associated video and you select it, you can opt to have Xbox automatically play the video for the song.

- **Playlists**—Here, you can access your playlists or create them. Playlists are a group of songs that are played together, sort of like compilation CDs. For example, you can create a playlist that contains your favorite songs, another to listen to while you're working out, and another to listen to while gaming. They're a great way for you to organize songs you like into whatever collections you want. The playlists you create automatically sync to your cloud collection so they are available from all of your devices. For more on playlists, see the "Create a Playlist" section later in this chapter.

- **Collection**—You can add favorite songs from the service to a personal collection, which show up here and are available from other Xbox Music-enabled devices.

- **Search**—Select this to launch the onscreen keyboard to search for the music you want.

Controlling the Music and Video Playback Menus

As any song or video is playing, you can pull up playback controls by pressing the Menu button on your controller. This also pulls up a menu of options, depending on where you're launching it from.

The playback options are the same whether you're listening to a song or watching a video. As expected, the left stick or D-pad moves between the various options, and the A button selects a highlighted option. Pressing the B button closes the playback menu. The following playback options are available:

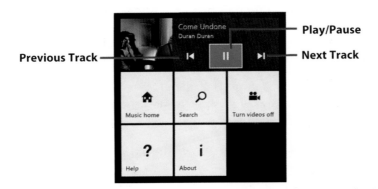

- **Play/Pause**—Select this icon to play or pause the current song.

- **Previous Track**—If there's a previous song/video, selecting this icon goes back one song/video. Otherwise, it restarts the current song/video.

- **Next Track**—If there's a next song/video, selecting this icon goes to the next song/video.

Another Way to Move Between Tracks

If you don't like a particular song, you don't have to launch the playback menu to move to the next one. Simply use your right trigger on your controller to go to the next track or your left trigger to go to the previous track.

- **Music Home**—This option brings you back to the Xbox Music Home screen. It's part of the menu when you launch it from Now Playing (what's currently playing).

Don't See Music Home?

This option appears only when you launch the playback menu from Now Playing. If you launch it from the Home screen, a Now Playing tile appears.

- **Search**—Select this option to launch the onscreen keyboard to search for music.

- **Now Playing**—This option only appears when you launch the playback menu from the Home screen. It exits the playback menu and brings you back into Now Playing.

- **Turn Videos On/Off**—You can opt to play videos if they're available. If this tile says Turn Videos Off, you have videos enabled. If you don't want to watch any music videos, this tile says Turn Videos On.

- **Help**—This option opens a Help menu that provides information about Xbox Music, how to play music and videos, how Xbox Music Pass works, and how you can manage your music collection.

- **About**—This option provides copyright and legal information for the music you have playing.

>>Go Further

USING YOUR VOICE IN XBOX MUSIC

You can also use your voice to get to Xbox Music and find music to listen to. In whatever app you're in, say "Xbox, Bing." Then say "Music." You now see a list of popular albums and genres. If you want to listen to the music you played last, you can say "Xbox, play music." If you're already on the Home screen of Xbox Music, say "Xbox select, search." However, you'll have to use your controller to enter a song, artist, or album.

You can also use a variety of voice shortcuts to control playback, including: "Pause," "Pause music," "Rewind," "Fast-forward," "Next song," "Previous song," and "Stop."

Create a Playlist

Playlists are a great way to enhance your music experience, and it can be fun putting together all kinds of compilations. To create a playlist, follow these steps:

1. Sign in to the account you want to use and, from the Home screen, launch the pre-pinned Xbox Music tile.

2. Select Playlists.

3. Select Create New Playlist.

4. Give your playlist a name and select Enter.

5. Select the playlist you just created.

6. Start adding music to your playlist by selecting Browse My Albums (only available if you've synced your collection) or Browse Catalog (brings you to the store). You can also go back to the Home screen and browse the various categories there, including Top Music and Featured.

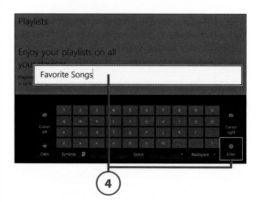

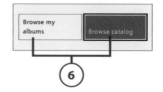

7. Once you find a song or album you want to add, select the + Add Song tile.

8. Select your playlist from the options and then keep adding songs to your playlist until you're happy with it.

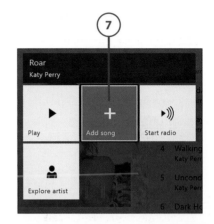

It's Not All Good

Incomplete Syncing

Any playlists you create in Xbox Music are automatically synced to your cloud-based collection, making them available from all of your enabled devices. However, if you have playlists that include music tracks from your own collection that are not available at the Xbox Music Store, your synced playlists won't contain those tracks. Streaming is not affected by what's available at the Xbox Music Store, so you can still listen to all of your music via this option.

Create a Radio Station

If you don't have any playlists, are in the mood to listen to a completely different genre of music, or want a more random, radio-like feel, you can instead create a radio station. In addition, with an Xbox Music Pass, you can avoid those pesky commercials. Follow these steps:

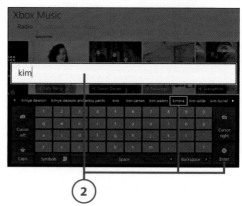

1. When in Xbox Music, go to the Radio tab and select Create Station.

2. Enter the name of an artist and select Enter or choose from the autogenerated options should you see the artist you want. For this example, enter "kim" and select the "kimbra" option.

3. Select the artist you want from the results. Xbox Music now picks music related to Kimbra and your radio channel starts playing.

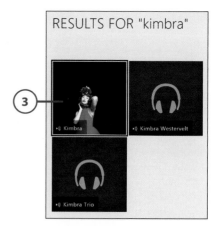

Streaming Your Personal Music Library

You can stream music to your Xbox One from a Windows 7 or later computer to Xbox Music. You can also do the same from most Android or iOS mobile devices using Skitfa, a free app that can stream from the mobile device, a network location, or a computer that is connected to the same network.

The music-streaming process works the same as it does for streaming videos and photos; see the sections "Stream Videos and Photos from Your Computer" and "Stream Videos from a Mobile Device," in Chapter 7, "Viewing Videos and Video Content." The only difference is that you run Xbox Music (rather than Xbox Video) and instead of selecting a video file, you select an audio file.

>>>Go Further

STREAMING YOUR OWN MUSIC WHILE PLAYING GAMES

If you want to listen to your own music while playing games, you need to stream your collection or select one of your playlists from Xbox Music. Thereafter, you need to go back to the Xbox One's Home screen, select the Snap tile, and then select the Xbox Music app. Once you start playing a game, you can go to the game's options menu and turn down or shut off the music for the game and then use the Snap app to start playing your music.

Playing Your Music CDs

If you don't want to sign up for Xbox Music or just want to listen to your own music, you can play your music CDs on your Xbox One. However, unlike on the Xbox 360, you can't rip music to your console's hard drive. The music CD needs to remain inserted in your console for it to play. This is a bummer if all your games are on disc, but if you have a digitally downloaded game you can simultaneously play your music CDs while gaming.

Before you can play your own music CDs, you'll need to install the Audio CD Player. At the time of this writing, the Audio CD Player only supports standard audio CDs. It doesn't support MP3s or nonstandard audio formats.

Install the Audio CD Player

Follow these steps to install the Audio CD Player:

1. When at the Home screen, insert a music CD into your Xbox One.

2. You now see an Audio CD Player screen. Select Install.

3. Once the download finishes, select Launch, or briefly hold the Xbox button on your controller when you see the onscreen launch notification.

4. Your music CD now starts playing.

Pin the Audio CD Player for Easy Access

If you plan to use the Audio CD Player a lot, be sure to pin it to the Home screen.

Understanding the Audio CD Player Interface

The Audio CD Player interface is very simple, as it only gives you basic controls and information on your CD's contents. The controls are the same as outlined in "Controlling the Music and Video Playback Menus" section earlier in this chapter. For quick reference, the Audio CD Player's functionality is also shown in the image below.

When a song is highlighted, press A to play it

Harem
Sarah Brightman, 2003-05-20, Contemporary Pop

1. Harem (Cancao do Mar)   5:45
    Sarah Brightman
2. What A Wonderful World   3:40
    Sarah Brightman
3. It's A Beautiful Day   3:56
    Sarah Brightman
4. What You Never Know   3:24
    Sarah Brightman
5. The Journey Home   4:56
    Sarah Brightman
6. Free   3:45
    Sarah Brightman
7. Mysterious Days   5:17
    Sarah Brightman

Previous Track
Play/Pause
Next Track   **More**

When you select More, the following options are available:

- **Turn Shuffle On**—Select to play your songs in random order.

- **Turn Repeat On**—Select to have your CD repeat once it's done looping through.

- **Go Back**—Select to go back to the Audio CD Player Interface.

Plays songs randomly   Turn shuffle on

Repeats your CD   Turn repeat on

Returns you to the interface   Go back

**Play your personal
videos or slideshows of
your photos**

**Access your Upload
Studio game clips**

In this chapter, you discover OneDrive, Microsoft's multiplatform file-hosting service that enables you to access your photos and videos on your console, as well as share your Upload Studio clips with the world.

→ Getting to Know OneDrive on Xbox One
→ Integrating OneDrive from Other Devices

9

Managing Files with OneDrive

OneDrive, which had its name changed from SkyDrive after a trademark dispute with British Sky Broadcasting, is free online file storage that comes standard with a Microsoft account, including the account used to log in to your Xbox One. With the OneDrive app for the Xbox One, you can view your photos and videos on your TV, including those shared from others. If you add game clips to OneDrive from Upload Studio, you can share them with your friends from the OneDrive website, or upload those videos to popular social networks like YouTube, Facebook, and Twitter. OneDrive functionality is also available for Windows and Macintosh computers; Android, Apple, and Windows mobile devices; and even the Xbox 360, so you'll almost never be without access to your files.

Getting to Know OneDrive on Xbox One

Like many of the other great features on the Xbox One, using OneDrive requires an Xbox Live Gold membership (see Chapter 3, "Examining Xbox Live"). Whether you have OneDrive access from a previous Microsoft sign-up or if this is your first time with the service through your Xbox One, the base amount of cloud storage space is 7GB. By referring friends, completing certain activities, buying certain products, or outright purchasing additional storage space (see https://onedrive.live.com/about/en-us/plans/ for upgrade options), this total can increase to the hundreds of gigabytes.

Although the Xbox One's app doesn't support all of the features found on some of the other platforms where OneDrive is available, it does let you view photos and videos, play slideshows, share Game DVR clips from Upload Studio, and even earn achievements, such as for viewing a certain number of photos. Of course, you can also use the Xbox One's Internet Explorer app (see Chapter 10, "Surfing with Internet Explorer") to go to OneDrive.com if you need to manage your files.

Install OneDrive

To use the OneDrive app, it must first be installed. To install OneDrive, do the following:

1. Select OneDrive from Pins. Alternately, you can select the app from the Apps section of the Store or by saying "Xbox, go to OneDrive."

2. Select Install.

3. Once installed, select Launch.

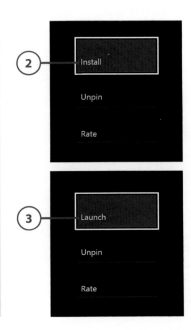

Taking Control of OneDrive

Once installed and launched, the app displays the main screen. If you have nothing installed to your OneDrive storage yet, then the image will look like this.

Photos and videos that others share with you

Your photo and videos folders

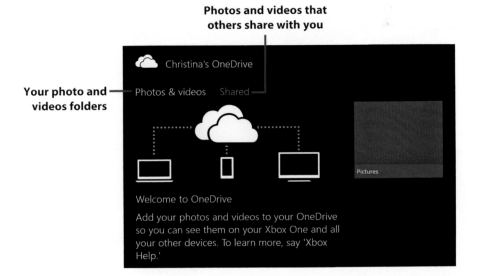

When you have content stored in your OneDrive account, either from Upload Studio or other sources, then the Pictures folder will cycle through thumbnails of available images and videos, similar to what is shown here.

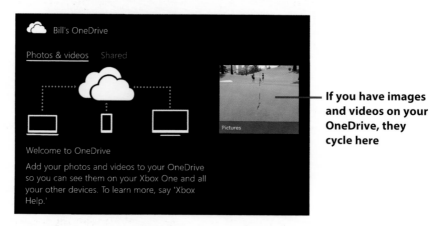

If you have images and videos on your OneDrive, they cycle here

There are two main sections that you can move between in the OneDrive app. Photos & Videos contains only your photos and videos, whereas Shared contains only those photos or videos others have expressly shared with you. You can move between the two headings with either the D-pad, left stick, or left and right bumpers. You can navigate with those same controls once a folder is selected with the A button.

When a folder with content is selected, the following options become available:

Sort **Slide Show** **Add to the OneGuide** **Current image number and total number of images**

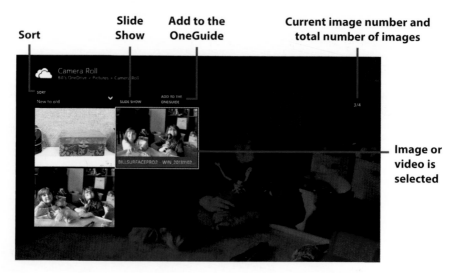

Image or video is selected

- **Sort**—Options include A to Z, Z to A, Old to New, New to Old (default), or a Custom sort order.

- **Slide Show**—Show the images or videos in the selected sort order on a loop.

- **Add to the OneGuide**—Create a shortcut to the folder on OneGuide (see "Working with OneGuide" in Chapter 7, "Viewing Videos and Video Content").

Once you highlight a file and select it with the A button, it either displays full screen if it's an image or starts playing if it's a video. Once an image or video is displayed, the following controller options become available:

- **A button**—Play a slideshow starting with the image selected. You can also choose the Slide Show button. The slideshow automatically loops, restarting at the beginning once it reaches the end of the folder's contents. If a video is playing, standard video playback controls apply (refer to "Controlling Playback" under "Enjoying TV Shows, Music Videos, and Movies with Xbox Video" in Chapter 7).

Want to Loop the Same Video?
To loop the same video, put two copies of the video in the same folder.

- **Left bumper**—Go to the previous image.

- **Right bumper**—Go to the next image.

- **Left trigger**—Zoom out on a photo.

- **Right trigger**—Zoom in on a photo.

- **Left stick or D-pad**—Display the playback overlay and move left and right between the Rewind, Pause/Play, and Fast Forward options. Press the A button to activate the highlighted option.

- **Right stick**—Move around the photo when you're zoomed in.

- **X button**—Switch between fitting a photo to your screen and filling the whole screen.

- **B button**—Go back to the previous screen.

- **Menu button**—Display the OneDrive app options, which are described below.

It's Not All Good

Is Your Video Choppy?

If your Internet or network connection is not fast enough, certain large, high-quality video files might have trouble playing smoothly. If this happens, find ways to improve your connectivity (see "Networking Enhancements" under "Accessorizing Your Xbox One" in Chapter 4, "Personalizing Your Xbox One Experience," for some options) or try saving the video at a lower resolution.

When you press the Menu button, the following options are available:

- **Switch profile**—Switch Xbox One profiles, which changes which OneDrive folders you can access.

- **Help**—Display helpful OneDrive information.

Integrating OneDrive from Other Devices

To see, add, and manage all of your files, you need to log in with your Microsoft account to OneDrive.com or use the OneDrive app from a computer or mobile device.

OneDrive functionality is preinstalled on computers and mobile devices with Windows 8 or later. For Windows tablets, you can also set the app to automatically back up your camera roll. For computers with Windows Vista or later, and Macintosh OS X (Lion or later), you can download the app from the OneDrive.com website.

For Google Android and Apple iOS mobile devices, you can download the app from the Google Play store and Apple App Store, respectively. Windows Phone devices have the app built-in. For all of these devices, you can also set the app to automatically back up your camera roll.

For the Xbox 360, you need to download and install the app from Apps. Functionality on the Xbox 360 is the same as that on the Xbox One save for its lack of Game DVR and Upload Studio integration.

Once you've got access to OneDrive in the places where you need it, it's time to start setting it up for your own personal needs and make use of it.

Change Folder Types

If a folder with pictures or videos in it doesn't show up on Xbox One, the folder type might need to be changed. To change folder types from the OneDrive website, follow these steps:

1. Sign in at OneDrive.com.

2. Select the folder.

3. Select the Details pane.

4. Under the Information panel, select Change to the far right of Folder Type.

5.   Under Change Folder Type, select Pictures.

6.   Select Save. The folder and any images or videos will now be visible within the Xbox One's OneDrive app.

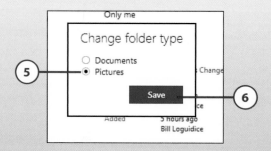

Add Files

With the exception of Upload Studio, you can't directly add files from your Xbox One's OneDrive app to One-Drive. For that, you should sign in at OneDrive.com and select Upload. To add files through the OneDrive web-site, follow these steps:

Automatic Uploads

On some devices, including some mobile phones and tablets, you can set your camera roll to automatically upload new photos to your OneDrive account.

1.   Select Upload. (Note that you must already have signed in to OneDrive.com.)

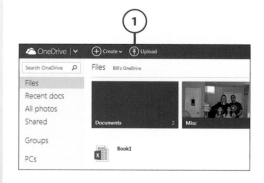

2. Select a file or files. If you're using a Windows or Linux computer, you can select more than one file by holding down the Ctrl key or, if you want to select a sequential block of files, by holding the Shift key. On a Macintosh computer, the only difference is using the Command key instead of Ctrl.

3. Select Open.

4. The file or files start uploading.

5. After the file or files have finished uploading, they appear in your list of OneDrive files. You can then access these files, depending on their type, using the Xbox One OneDrive app.

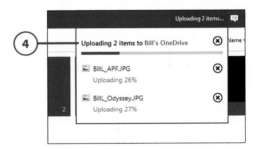

Share Files

You can share OneDrive files or folders with other people you specify through a shared link or by publishing directly to Facebook. To share your files in this manner so that they appear under Shared for your friends, sign in to OneDrive.com from your computer. From there, follow these steps:

1. Select the folder, file, or files you'd like to share.

2. Select the Details pane.

3. Select Share or Share Folder under the Sharing panel.

4. Select Invite People.

5. Enter a list of recipients in the To field and, if you like, add a short message to let them know what you've sent.

6. Select Share.

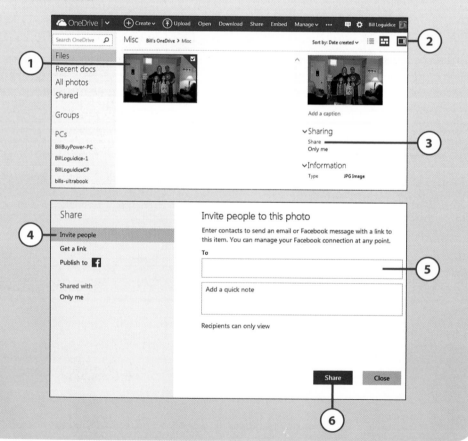

OTHER WAYS TO SHARE

From the Share window, you can also choose Get a Link to get a link that you can then copy and paste anywhere you want. Or, you can use the Publish To option to send photos or videos to a new or existing Facebook album.

You can further refine most of these options to View Only, which means anyone with the link can see the files you share but not make any changes to them; Edit, which means anyone with the link can edit the files you share; or Public, meaning anyone can search for and view your public files even if you don't share the link.

Although you can share files directly to Facebook using the Share function from OneDrive.com, there are no such options for other social network or video sharing websites. By selecting Get a Link and setting the display option to Public, you can then copy and paste the link to Twitter, Facebook, Google+, or any other social network or blog of your choice.

If you'd like to upload an actual file to one of these services, for instance, a video to YouTube or Facebook, select the Download option on the OneDrive.com website when your file, files, or folder is selected. This downloads the file to your computer, where you can then upload it to any of these services like you normally would. Although your editing options will be limited, you can also use the Xbox One's YouTube app (see "YouTube" in Chapter 7, "Viewing Videos and Video Content") to directly upload your saved Game DVR clips.

Report Inappropriate Sharing

To see photos and videos that are shared with you, look under Shared. Occasionally, spam images or other unwanted materials might be shared with you. If it's not something you can resolve with a friend, then report the image by doing the following after signing in to OneDrive.com:

1. Select Shared.

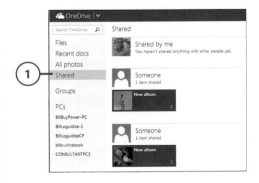

2. Select the photo or video.

3. Under Manage, select Report Abuse.

4. Select the type of abuse and write any comments you might have.

5. Click the Report Abuse button when you're satisfied with the report.

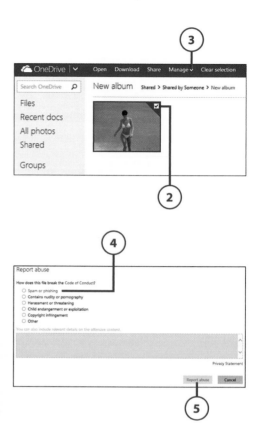

Learn about Internet Explorer's capabilities on your Xbox One

Discover tabbed browsing and how to save favorite web pages so that you can easily access them

In this chapter, you learn how to use Internet Explorer on your Xbox One.

→ Understanding Internet Explorer on Xbox One

→ Adjusting Internet Explorer Settings

→ Learning the Internet Explorer Interface

→ Navigating Web Pages

Surfing with Internet Explorer

Internet Explorer is Microsoft's web browser. If you have a Microsoft Windows operating system on your computer or laptop, chances are that you've already used Internet Explorer in some capacity. But the neat thing about having Internet Explorer on your Xbox One console is that you can use it to explore the Web right on your TV and can even use your voice, gestures, or SmartGlass to easily navigate your favorite sites.

In this chapter, you learn how to set up and make the most of Internet Explorer on your Xbox One. You also learn how you can use Bing, Microsoft's search engine, to locate the content you're looking for.

Understanding Internet Explorer on Xbox One

If you've used Internet Explorer on Xbox 360, you'll find three key improvements that enhance the user experience on Xbox One:

- **Supports modern web standards**—Internet Explorer on the Xbox One supports modern web standards, including HTML5 and CSS3, enabling more sites to function and look great on your TV.

- **More navigation options**—In addition to using your controller, you can use your voice or gestures to control Internet Explorer. You can also make use of SmartGlass, which enables you to navigate Internet Explorer with a tablet or mobile device instead of a controller, as well as to transfer web pages between your mobile device and your Xbox One. For more on SmartGlass, turn to Chapter 11, "Looking Through the SmartGlass."

- **Additional browser features**—Internet Explorer on your Xbox One includes many features that were previously only available on a Windows PC, including website pinning, multiple tabs, InPrivate browsing, Smart-Screen, Cookie blocking, and Do Not Track.

Before you can start using Internet Explorer on your Xbox One, you need to have an Xbox Live Gold membership. In addition, although Internet Explorer comes preinstalled on your Xbox One, you need to set it up before you can use it.

Had an Xbox 360?

If you previously used an Xbox 360 and pinned or saved any sites to your Favorites in Internet Explorer, they'll automatically be pulled forward to your Xbox One, so no need to hunt for them again on your Xbox One.

Set Up Internet Explorer

Setting up Internet Explorer on your Xbox One is easy because it's already preinstalled. You basically just need to set your preferences and you're good to go. Follow these steps:

1. Sign in to your account and select the Internet Explorer app from the Home screen (A). If you do not see it on the Home screen, select the My Games & Apps tile (B), select Apps (C), and then select the Internet Explorer tile (D).

2. Select a setting for Turn On SmartScreen Filter. The authors recommend that you keep this filter turned on, as it helps detect phishing websites and can help protect you from downloading or installing malware.

Learning About SmartScreen

If you want to learn more about the SmartScreen filter, select Learn More, and then select SmartScreen for Safe Browsing.

3. Select a setting for Turn On Do Not Track. This is another feature that helps protect your privacy by blocking online tracking.

4. Select a setting for Send My Personal Browsing History to Microsoft. Check this option if you'd like to share your personal browsing history with Microsoft to help improve its products. Leaving this unchecked doesn't have any effect on your web browsing experience.

5. Select Next to continue.

6. Press the View button on the controller to access the address bar.

7. You are now in Internet Explorer and can start browsing; see the sections "Learning the Internet Explorer Interface" and "Navigating Web Pages" for more on the interface and how to navigate it, respectively.

>>>Go Further

UNDERSTANDING COOKIES

Every time you use the Web, companies are collecting and storing information about you and your web activity by creating a small text file or computer ID when your browser loads a website. These bits of data are known as *cookies*. Many cookies are harmless and useful. For example, they might ensure automatic logins, authentication when you want to access a website again, and store the ordering information needed for online shopping carts. Others may only be beneficial to the company and threaten your Internet security, such as by installing adware or spyware applications on your hard drive. So for this option, you'll need to decide whether convenience or privacy is more important to you.

Grasping the Internet Explorer Menu Options

When you're in Internet Explorer and on any web page, you can access a menu of website-specific (appears in the gray area) and Internet Explorer-specific (appears in the blue area) menu options by selecting the Menu button on your controller. This menu includes the following options:

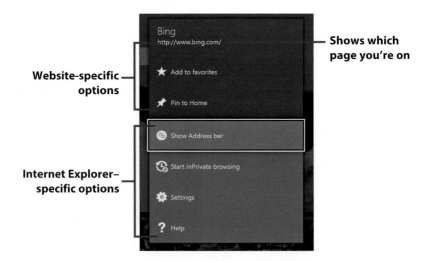

- **Add to Favorites**—Above this option, you see the name of the website you're on, along with the site's uniform resource locator (URL). If you want to favorite this site, then select this option. Once you do, the website is added to your Favorites, which is accessible when you select the Show Address Bar option.

- **Pin to Home**—Select this option if you want to pin the website you're on to the Pins section of the Home screen.

- **Show Address Bar**—This option pulls up the Internet Explorer interface, from which you can conduct searches using Bing and access a variety of other options. See the "Learning the Internet Explorer Interface" section later in this chapter for more on what you'll find here.

- **Start InPrivate Browsing**—Select this option if you don't want to leave a trace of your web browsing activity on your console. This option helps prevent your browsing history, temporary Internet files, form data, cookies, and usernames and passwords from being retained by the browser. If you select this option and want to resume normal browsing, simply press the Menu button again and then select End InPrivate Browsing.

- **Settings**—Go here to delete your history and adjust your general and privacy settings for Internet Explorer. For more on Internet Explorer settings, turn to the "Adjusting Internet Explorer Settings" section of this chapter.

- **Help**—Select this option if you're looking for additional information and tips on how to use Internet Explorer on your console.

Adjusting Internet Explorer Settings

Once you set up Internet Explorer, you might want to tweak some settings before you start browsing the Web. In addition, the options you enabled when you set up Internet Explorer appear checked off here, and you can modify these if you want.

To adjust your settings, press the Menu button on your controller when in Internet Explorer and then select Settings. The following options are now available to you:

Select to delete your browsing history

Opens when you select the Learn More option

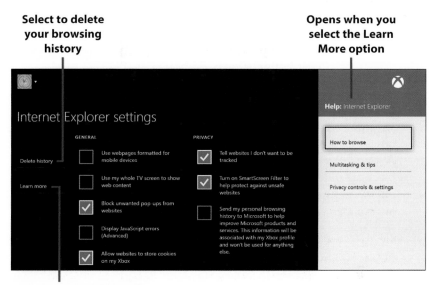

Select to access the Internet Explorer Help menu that appears to the far right

- **Delete History**—Select this option if you want to delete your browsing history. Keep in mind if you delete this, you might also delete useful stored information, such as saved web passwords.

- **Learn More**—Select this option to pull up the same information as the Help option when you press the Menu button while in Internet Explorer. Select this option if you need more information on Internet Explorer settings.

- **Use Webpages Formatted for Mobile Devices**—If you find a web page that's not displaying properly on your console, consider selecting this option. In the event that a mobile device version of the page is available, it might display better on your Xbox One, as these pages are designed and streamlined to be compatible on more devices.

- **Use My Whole TV Screen to Show Web Content**—If this option is not checked, a black border appears around the web page. If checked, this is like pressing F11 while in a web browser on your computer; it fills the whole screen with the web page. On some displays, going full screen can cut off a portion of a web page's content on the outer edges, so be sure to choose the option that works best for your specific setup.

- **Block Unwanted Pop-ups from Websites**—Pop-ups are little windows that can suddenly appear onscreen when you're perusing a website. They are often associated with advertisements and can quickly clutter the screen, so it is better to keep this option enabled.

- **Display JavaScript Errors (Advanced)**—If you want to get into the technical details of why a website doesn't work, you can enable this option.

- **Allow Websites to Store Cookies on My Xbox**—Cookies are small pieces of data sent from the websites you visit to your web browser, where they're stored. They contain information about your activity. For example, they'll store items in a shopping cart when you're shopping online and save your login information for certain websites.

- **Privacy**—For more information on all of the available options here, see step 2 in the "Setting Up Internet Explorer" section earlier in this chapter.

Learning the Internet Explorer Interface

Internet Explorer provides a full-screen browser experience. This enables you to focus on the content you're interested in, rather than having the screen cluttered with nonessential items.

After you set up Internet Explorer, the next time you access it, you're brought to Bing.com, which is set as the default home page. To get to the Internet Explorer interface, just press the Menu button on your controller and then select Show Address Bar.

The following Internet Explorer options are now available to you:

Sign in to a different account

Access your tabbed web pages

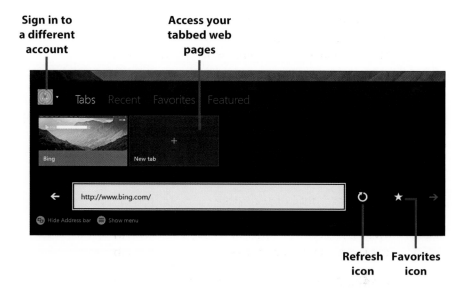

Refresh icon   **Favorites icon**

- **Sign In**—Select this icon to sign in a different Xbox Live Gold member; remember, unless an individual has Xbox Live Gold, he or she can't access Internet Explorer.

- **Tabs**—Select this option to enable tabbed browsing, meaning you can view multiple pages/search results in one window by loading the desired websites into separate "tabbed" sections. For more on this, turn to the "Work with Tabs" section next.

- **Recent**—Select this option to access the web pages you recently viewed.

- **Favorites**—Select this option to quickly access your web pages that you've made Favorites. For instructions on how to do this, turn to the "Save and Delete Favorites" section later in this chapter.

- **Featured**—Select this option to view sites and applications that Microsoft is highlighting.

- **Bing Search Bar**—Click in the Bing search bar to use the onscreen keyboard to conduct a search or enter a URL.

Work with Tabs

Tabs can make your web browsing experience much more enjoyable and manageable, as they keep the web pages you're interested in easily acces-sible. To add tabs, follow these steps:

1. From Internet Explorer, select the Menu button and then select Show Address Bar.

2. Scroll to New Tab and press the A button to select it. There is now a blank page available, which is filled by whatever website you choose.

3. Go to the search bar and press the A button.

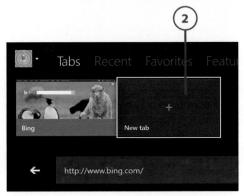

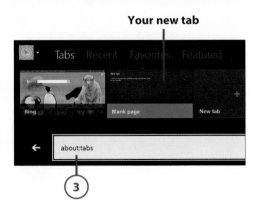

Your new tab

4. Use the onscreen keyboard to enter a term or web page of your choosing; as you type, you might see Suggestions appear at the top of the screen. If you see what you want listed there, scroll to it and press the A button. Otherwise, finish entering your term/destination and then select Enter.

5. When you're finished perusing the website, select the View button on your controller to add it to the tab. If you select the B button to go back, it won't be added to the tab.

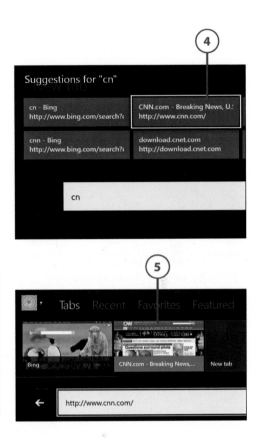

DELETING TABS AND OPENING ITEMS IN NEW TABS

To delete a particular tab, simply scroll to the tab you want to delete, press the Menu button on your controller, and then select Close Tab. If you're on a website and find an item you want to open in a new tab, simply press the Menu button on your controller and select Open in New Tab. If you don't want to save it to a tab, but just open it, select Open.

Save and Delete Favorites

In addition to making a website a Favorite via the Internet Explorer menu (see the "Add to Favorites" bullet point in the "Grasping the Internet Explorer Menu Options" section earlier in this chapter), you can do the following:

1. Go to the website you want to add to your Favorites.

2. Select the View button on your controller to get back to the address bar, where the website is listed in the Bing search bar, and select the star icon.

3. The item now appears under Favorites. To delete an item from Favorites, proceed to the next step.

4. Select the item you want to delete, and then press the Menu button on your controller.

5. Select Remove from Favorites.

Navigating Web Pages

Although navigating the Web with a controller may be less than ideal, Microsoft has provided pretty intuitive controls to accomplish this task. You can use the following basic controls to navigate web pages with your controller:

- **Left and right bumpers**—The left bumper zooms out whereas the right bumper zooms in so that you can get a closer look.

- **Menu button**—Opens a menu of options, such as enabling you to add an item to Favorites, pin it to Home, or open it in another tab.

- **View button**—Returns you to the Address Bar screen where you can access your tabs, recently viewed items, favorite items, and items featured by Microsoft.

- **B button**—Brings you back to the previous screen.

- **A button**—Selects an item.

- **D-pad**—Quickly scrolls through chunks of text.

- **Left stick**—Moves a cursor left and right. Pressing it in also zooms the page in and out with each press.

- **Right stick**—Moves a cursor up and down.

You can also use Kinect to control web pages via gestures and voice. For more information on how to achieve this, turn to the "Understanding Kinect Controls" section in Chapter 2, "Navigating Your Xbox One's Dashboard and Settings." Another great way to control web pages is via SmartGlass, which is discussed in Chapter 11.

Use the Xbox One SmartGlass app from a variety of mobile devices

Interact with any accessible Xbox One console on the same network

Pin your favorites to sync with your console

Take complete control of your Xbox One console

In this chapter, you learn about SmartGlass, a powerful app that turns your mobile device into a second screen that intelligently interacts with your Xbox One.

→ Downloading and Installing the SmartGlass App
→ Using the SmartGlass App

11

Looking Through the SmartGlass

Xbox One SmartGlass turns your Windows, Google Android, or Apple iOS mobile device into a powerful second screen and controller for your console. Take control of your media and snapped apps, get game help, and more. When you're on the go, check out your achievements and messages, search for content, and pin your favorites, which will be waiting for you on your Xbox One when you sign in. In this chapter, you learn how to tap the potential of this impressive interactive experience.

Coming Soon
An update coming in the latter part of 2014, perhaps by the time you read this, will give SmartGlass even more control over your Xbox One, television, and cable or satellite receiver box. This update includes an enhanced virtual remote control, setting new recordings and watching recorded content from your DVR, and showing your most recently watched channels.

Downloading and Installing the SmartGlass App

Like the original Xbox SmartGlass app for the Xbox 360, the Xbox One SmartGlass app works on a wide variety of devices. For Windows devices, it runs on Windows 8 and Windows RT or greater tablets and PCs, as well as Windows Phone 8 or greater, and is available from the respective Windows Store. For Google Android devices, it runs on most smartphones and tablets that run Android 4.x or greater and that have access to the Google Play store. For Apple iOS 6.x or greater devices, it runs on iPod touch 4th generation or greater, iPhone 3GS or greater, iPad 2 or greater, and all versions of the iPad mini, and is available from the App Store on iTunes.

It's Not All Good

Performance Issues?

Xbox One SmartGlass performance varies based on the speed of your network connection and the processing power of your computer or mobile device.

The two sections that follow provide examples for procuring the app on Windows 8 and iOS devices, respectively. The procedures are similar for other platforms.

Download and Install on a Windows 8 Device

To download and install the Xbox One SmartGlass app on your Windows 8 device, do the following:

1. Select the Store icon from the Windows 8 Start screen.

Searching for Store

From the Start screen, you can also just type the word "store" and, when it appears in search results, select the Store app.

2. Type "xbox one smartglass" in the Search field and press Enter or tap on the Search icon.

3. Tap on the Xbox One SmartGlass icon.

4. Tap on Install to download the app.

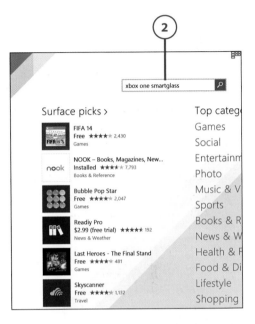

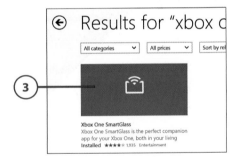

5. Once installed, the Xbox One SmartGlass app is available in your list of Apps and can be accessed like other apps by tapping on its icon.

Download and Install on an iOS Device

To download and install the Xbox One SmartGlass app on your iOS device, do the following:

1. Tap on the App Store icon.

2. Type "xbox one smartglass" in the Search field.

3. Tap on "xbox one smartglass" under Results.

4. Tap on the install icon to download the app.

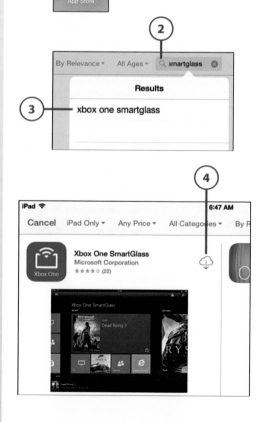

5. Once installed, tap Open. In the future, you can start the app like other apps by tapping on its icon on your Apps screen.

Using the SmartGlass App

There are a variety of ways to put SmartGlass to work. You can use it as a Remote Control to tell your Xbox One what to do. This isn't particularly useful for games, but it's great when paired with the Internet Explorer web browser and for entering passwords, sending messages, and so on.

As a second screen, SmartGlass exposes even more potential. Using this feature, game developers can enable you to interact with content in even more ways than limiting you to what's happening on the TV. Think of an RPG that lets you manage inventory on your tablet without cluttering up your TV, or a sports game that lets you see stats or lineups without having to pause and open a menu.

Before a SmartGlass app can work with your Xbox One, however, you need to make sure that your console is set to allow a connection.

Tell Your Xbox to Talk to SmartGlass

To allow the connection, do the following:

1. From the Home screen, press the Menu button on your controller and select Settings.

2. Select Preferences.

3. Under SmartGlass Connections, select either From any SmartGlass Device or Only from Profiles Signed in on This Xbox, depending upon your preference.

Disabling SmartGlass

If Don't Allow SmartGlass Connections is selected, the SmartGlass app can't connect to your Xbox. Refer to "Changing the Console Settings" in Chapter 2, "Navigating Your Xbox One's Dashboard and Settings," for more information.

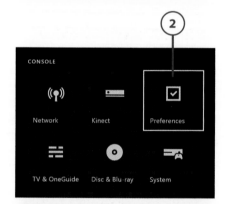

>>>Go Further

COMPLETING THE PROCESS

Once the Xbox One SmartGlass app is installed on your mobile device, you'll be asked to sign in with your Microsoft ID. This is the same login you use for your Xbox One. For SmartGlass to see the intended Xbox One console, both devices must be on the same network, with the console already set to allow the intended connection type.

Connect SmartGlass to Your Console

To connect SmartGlass to your console, turn on your Xbox One, open the Smart-Glass app using your platform of choice, and follow these steps:

1. Select Connect to Xbox One. If your console is powered on and connected to your home net-work, you should see it appear in SmartGlass.

How SmartGlass Looks

Save for differences in screen orienta-tion, Xbox One SmartGlass function-ality is fairly consistent across the various devices the app is available on. As such, we selected the Apple iPad version of the app to demon-strate the representative example used here.

2. Select your console to connect SmartGlass to it. Once you select an Xbox One console, you have the option of establishing a connection automatically the next time you run the app.

3. Select Connect to establish a connection and display the Home screen.

Connecting Automatically

Note that, when connecting, there is a Connect Automatically checkbox. If you don't want SmartGlass to automatically connect to your Xbox as soon as you launch the app, you should de-select this checkbox.

If your console doesn't appear, tap this link to search for its IP address

Find Your Xbox One's IP Address

If your console is on the same network as your device and the connection type you're attempting is allowed, and you still don't see the console listed, you can enter its IP address. To find your console's IP address, do the following from your Xbox One:

1. From the Home screen, press the Menu button on your controller and select Settings.

2. Select Network.

3. Select Advanced Settings.

4. Write down your console's specific IP address, which you'll need to enter in the SmartGlass app. (Refer to step 2 of the previous task, "Connect SmartGlass to Your Console.")

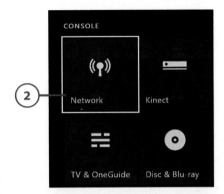

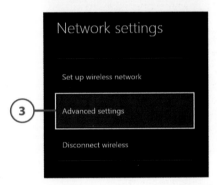

Using SmartGlass without Your Xbox

When you launch SmartGlass, instead of connecting to your Xbox One, you can choose to skip this process, which allows you to browse the app without being connected and perform simple activities like adding and removing pins. Any changes you make here sync with your console the next time you sign in.

Select your Xbox One console name from the list

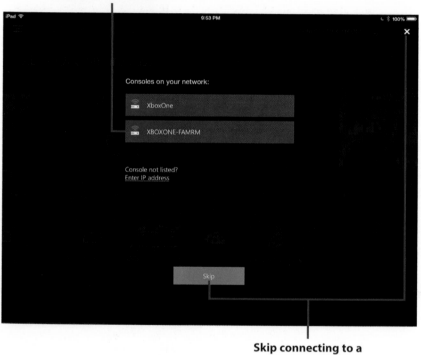

Skip connecting to a console and browse the app instead

Getting to Know the SmartGlass App

Once connected, the following features are available from the Home screen:

- **Menu Bar**—This area provides three main options: Main Menu (described later in this section), Connect (connect or disconnect from a console), and Search, which is equivalent to a Bing search on your Xbox One, enabling you to search for games, music, movies, and TV shows.

Main menu

Connect

Search

- **My Pins**—This area functions as a mirror of the pins you have available when signed in to your Xbox One console. Tapping a pin provides the following options: Play on Xbox One, Play in Snap, Details, and Unpin. If you're not connected to your Xbox One, changes to what's pinned will sync the next time you sign in to your console.

Tap a pin to display options

- **Recent**—Similar to the Home screen on your Xbox One console, this area displays your recently opened apps and games. Tapping a tile provides the following options: Play on Xbox One, Play in Snap (if supported), Details, and Unpin.

The app or game currently running on the Xbox One

Other recent apps and games

- **Featured**—Just like Featured on the Xbox One console, this area displays content that Microsoft is presently highlighting (advertising). Tap an item to display its Details screen, which includes an option to pin the item to My Pins.

Tap an item to display its Details screen

- **Information and Remote Bar**—This bar describes what is presently playing on the Xbox One and provides options for controlling the volume on your television or sound system if configured on your console. It also provides a full-screen remote control, which is like a virtual wireless controller, for taking control of your console. (See the "Using SmartGlass as a Remote Control" section later in this chapter.) Media controls will also appear in this area when appropriate for a particular app or function.

Volume control

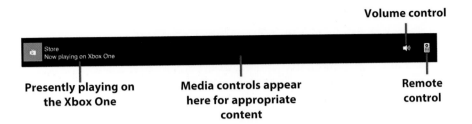

**Presently playing on
the Xbox One**

**Media controls appear
here for appropriate
content**

**Remote
control**

Tapping the Main Menu icon reveals the following options:

**Tap an option
to select it**

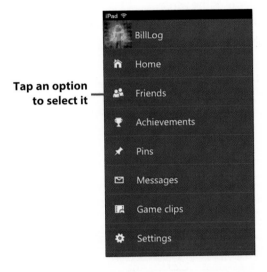

- **Home**—Returns to the app's Home screen

- **Friends**—Displays your Friends list and activity feed; similar to the Xbox One's Friends app (see Chapter 6, "Making the Social Connection")

- **Achievements**—Displays both your account's achievements as well as the achievements of your friends

- **Pins**—Allows you to add and remove pins; a dedicated version of My Pins

- **Messages**—Enables you to view any messages received or send messages via your mobile device's virtual keyboard

- **Game Clips**—Enables you to play any of the game clips from your Game DVR sessions

- **Settings**—Provides an option to keep your device from locking while the SmartGlass app is open, as well as displays app version and other miscellaneous information

Using SmartGlass as a Remote Control

The Xbox One's Home screen, apps, and live TV can all be controlled with the full-screen remote that either appears automatically or is selected from the Remote Control icon. Taps activate the virtual equivalents of the wireless controller's face buttons, while finger swipes mimic the D-pad or left stick. Tapping one of the media controls, when available, activates the appropriate function, such as Play or Fast Forward.

Virtual equivalents of the wireless controller's face buttons

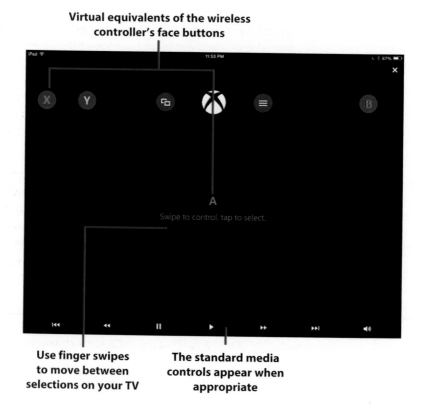

Swipe to control, tap to select.

Use finger swipes to move between selections on your TV

The standard media controls appear when appropriate

The SmartGlass app only presents the text input keyboard if you're in the full-screen remote, which is selected from the Remote Control icon. Even if a text input box is displayed on the TV, you might still need to tap on the Smart-Glass app's remote screen to put the console, and SmartGlass itself, into Text Input mode. If the keyboard is not visible on your TV, SmartGlass doesn't display text input.

If the console is displaying the onscreen keyboard but the SmartGlass app is still showing the full-screen remote, tap the onscreen B button to dismiss the keyboard, then tap the onscreen A button to once again display the console keyboard.

Certain Xbox One apps have extended functions when the full-screen remote is displayed. For instance, Internet Explorer lets you control the equivalent of a mouse pointer with your finger, and also provides a dedicated address bar for quicker URL entry.

Using SmartGlass as a Second Screen

Videos and games that display the SmartGlass logo support second screen functionality when both the video or game and the SmartGlass app are running. For instance, when you're watching television shows and movies that support it, Xbox SmartGlass turns into a companion app, providing extended information relevant to what's happening on the screen. SmartGlass companion experiences include everything from the names and biographies of specific actors or characters to real-time journals and maps that help you keep track of what's going on where in a program at a specific time.

For games that support SmartGlass, the possibilities are even more interesting. For instance, in *Dead Rising 3*, you're provided with exclusive missions that unlock apps within the SmartGlass app, such as the ability to call in air strikes, drone support, or area-wide flares for distracting the masses of zombies bearing down on you. The SmartGlass app can also be used to locate specific types of items and abandoned storefronts, which is a great way for a friend to play a supporting role, such as for locating useful weapons or setting critical waypoints for mission objectives.

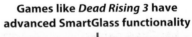

Games like *Dead Rising 3* have advanced SmartGlass functionality

Index

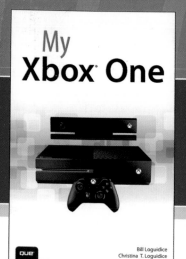

My
Xbox One

Bill Loguidice
Christina T. Loguidice

QUE

DISCARD

Safari
Books Online

FREE
Online Edition

Your purchase of *My Xbox One* includes access to a free online edition for 45 days through the **Safari Books Online** subscription service. Nearly every Que book is available online through **Safari Books Online**, along with thousands of books and videos from publishers such as Addison-Wesley Professional, Cisco Press, Exam Cram, IBM Press, O'Reilly Media, Prentice Hall, Sams, and VMware Press.

Safari Books Online is a digital library providing searchable, on-demand access to thousands of technology, digital media, and professional development books and videos from leading publishers. With one monthly or yearly subscription price, you get unlimited access to learning tools and information on topics including mobile app and software development, tips and tricks on using your favorite gadgets, networking, project management, graphic design, and much more.

Activate your FREE Online Edition at
informit.com/safarifree

STEP 1:   Enter the coupon code: LVBAHAA.

STEP 2:   New Safari users, complete the brief registration form.
Safari subscribers, just log in.

If you have difficulty registering on Safari or accessing the online edition,
please e-mail customer-service@safaribooksonline.com

Addison
Wesley

Adobe Press

ALPHA

Cisco Press

Press
FINANCIAL TIMES

IBM
Press.

Microsoft
Press

New
Riders

O'REILLY

Peachpit
Press

PRENTICE
HALL

QUE

Redbooks

SAMS

SSas
Publishing

vmware PRESS

WILEY

WROX